IMAGES OF HEAVEN
Reflections on Glory

Section Introductions by *CALVIN MILLER*

IMAGES OF

HEAVEN

REFLECTIONS ON GLORY

Harold Shaw Publishers
Wheaton, Illinois

Cover and inside design by David LaPlaca
Compiled by Lil Copan and Anna Trimiew
Cover photo copyright © 1996 by Patricia Sgrignoli

02 01 00 99 98 97 96

10 9 8 7 6 5 4 3 2 1

A NOTE TO THE READER

In order to provide more accessible readings, we have made certain changes in this book. We have frequently eliminated ellipses, changed awkward spellings, and where more extensive changes were made, have added the word *adapted*. These changes have been slight; the essential work of these writers remains clear in these pages.

For selections taken from quote books—or anything other than the given author's primary work—we have not noted the original source or translator's name unless they were provided in these sources.

When no source is cited in the sidebar, quotes were taken from the section text.

May the following selections provide you glimpses of heaven as you follow the pilgrim's path toward the eternal kingdom.

CONTENTS

ACROSS THE CANYON OF ETERNITY: THE ROAD TO GLORY

ENTERING THE FAIR COUNTRY: THE ETERNAL KINGDOM

THE SOUND OF STRONG THUNDER: INFINITE PRAISES

ACKNOWLEDGMENTS

We have sought to secure permissions for all copyrighted material in this book. Where copyright holders could not be located or acknowledgment was inadvertently omitted, the publisher expresses its regret.

Grateful acknowledgment is made to the following for permission to include their works in this anthology (listed in alphabetical order according to author):

"Arrival," from *Shaker, Why Don't You Sing?* by Maya Angelou. Copyright © 1983 by Maya Angelou. Reprinted by permission of Random House, Inc.

"There and Now," © 1995, and "The Third Day," © 1993 by Rachel Landrum Crumble. Used by permission of the author.

W. E. B. Du Bois's prayers are reprinted from PRAYERS FOR DARK PEOPLE, by W. E. B. Du Bois, ed. by Herbert Aptheker (Amherst: University of Massachusetts Press, 1980), copyright © 1980 by The University of Massachusetts Press.

Pearl excerpt, "As John the Apostle First Saw That Sight," translated by David Gould © 1995. Used by permission of the translator.

"Tambourines!" is taken from COLLECTED POEMS by Langston Hughes. Copyright © 1994 by the Estate of Langston Hughes. Reprinted by permission of Alfred A. Knopf Inc.

"Listen, Lord—A Prayer," "Go Down Death—A Funeral Sermon," "The Judgment Day," from GOD'S TROMBONES by James Weldon Johnson. Copyright 1927 The Viking Press, Inc., renewed © 1955 by Grace Nail Johnson. Used by permission of Viking Penguin, a division of Penguin Books USA Inc.

Excerpts taken from *The Last Battle* by C. S. Lewis are used by permission of HarperCollins *Publishers* Limited.

"Above All," excerpt from "A Letter of Saint Andrew the Dancer," © 1996 by Howard McCord. Used by permission of the author.

GLIMPSES OF

SPLENDOR

THE HOPE OF HEAVEN

INTRODUCTION
Calvin Miller

Those at Ravensbruck rejoiced
above the rumor that the
Allies were on their way.
Those about to die determined
they would live and strained
upon the housetops to catch
the first glimpse of the
color guard of freedom.

—Calvin Miller, *The Finale*

*W*hat is now
small and elusive
and distant will
soon be very real.

Glimpses of heaven are frequent. Here and there the real world of eternity shines through the scrim-cloth of the illusory now. Many have seen and reported the reality of heaven. The apostle John, for instance, saw heaven open (Revelation 19:11). He saw the glories of that everlasting realm which for most of us remains undefined.

When I was a pastor in the Midwest, I often took my children for vacations in Colorado. Our routine was predictable. As we traveled west, we would begin to search the horizon for our first glimpse of the Rocky Mountains. We always played this eager game the same way. We would squint our eyes and study the distant horizon, till it seemed our determined vision would glaze to blindness. Why squint? Because, when we narrow our eyes, their slitted accuracy becomes acute.

Were there really any mountains there? What was that irregular purple line that hugged the narrow flat horizon? Mountains? No. Just deflated clouds poured out like pancakes, too lazy and flat to stand up and be thunderheads. But what of those white-tipped purple clouds? Were they clouds? Were they mountains? No. No. No. But wait. Suddenly they were there, really there. They thrust themselves up in grand reality. Distant? Yes, but there. The Rockies really did exist.

At such moments we began to imagine what they would be like when our squinty glimpses gave way to being in them. Anticipation devoured the children. They knew they would soon be there among the up-thrust crags. The wonderland we longed to enjoy loomed large. Our minds cried, "Drive . . . drive . . . drive. For what is now small and elusive and distant will soon be very real."

When our children were in grammar school, we were surprised to find that our "landlord" had sold the house where we lived. Our church salary was small. We had not been able to accumulate the funds to make the necessary down-payment for the house that we needed to buy. Now that we knew we had to move and had no place to go we grew very depressed. At the height of our discouragement, I found a beautiful house, standing empty in a field of weeds. The old couple who had owned the house had died, each within a few months of the other. The lingering terminal illnesses that had claimed their lives had left them unable to do any yard work for a couple of years. The desolate, empty house was now for sale. The house would need a lot of work to make it livable. Still, the price was right. We had just enough money to manage the loan closure.

The day we moved out of our former home was traumatic. Our children were only babies when we had moved into the rental. We had a kind of romantic attachment to the old place where we had grown together as a family. We were reluctant to leave the thousand memories that hovered about the old place. We had become excited by glimpses of the better house that was now ours. We all believed in the coming glory of that deserted old relic of a house which stood reigning over

You first see heaven by squinting the eyes and moving toward what is only a glimpse.

its unkempt weed-patch. We could see one truth about the place. Its destiny was greater than its present existence.

The glimpse was liberating. Like travelers in search of the mountains, we squinted our eyes. We saw the vision of what the new place would be like once it was our home. In our reluctance to leave the house we had to vacate, I put my arm around my wife. I spoke to her the same words we had used when first we glimpsed the far, dim beauty of the Rockies, "Things are better further on."

How often do the Scriptures reckon with the distant vision in the squinting of the mind's eye? Julia Howe wrote, "I have seen him in the watchfires of a hundred circling camps. . . . I can read his righteous judgment in the dim and flaring lamps." The glimpse is always dim and flaring.

The glimpse of glory is what Jesus spoke about in John 14: "In my Father's house are many rooms; if it were not so, I would have told you. I am going there to prepare a place for you. And if I go and prepare a place you, I will come back and take you to be with me that you also may be where I am. You know the way to the place where I am going" (John 14:2-4, NIV).

But it was Thomas who said, "Lord, we don't have the foggiest idea of where you're going, so how can we know the way?"

It was then that Jesus said, in effect, "Thomas, heaven is not seen all at once as if it were a postcard of Yellowstone. You first see heaven by squinting the eyes and moving toward what is only a glimpse. Trust me, Thomas. The world ahead is real. Squint. Make your way toward what is yet indistinct on the horizon."

But Thomas protested, "What glimpse? What way?"

And Jesus answered: "I am the way and the truth and the life. No one comes to the Father except through me" (John 14:6, NIV).

The New Testament is really a book of glimpses. Heaven is really there. Here and there it thrusts up through the morning fog like the castles of Old Castile. Consider all the glimpses of these gallant lovers of God. See Stephen's glimpse:

> "Look," he said, "I see heaven open and the Son of Man standing at the right hand of God." (Acts 7:56, NIV)

Consider Paul's glimpse:

> Now we know that if the earthly tent we live in is destroyed, we have a building from God, an eternal house in heaven, not built by human hands. Meanwhile we groan, longing to be clothed with our heavenly dwelling. (1 Corinthians 5:1-2, NIV)

> I know a man in Christ who fourteen years ago was caught up to the third heaven. Whether it was in the body or out of the body I do not know—God knows. And I know that this man—whether in the body or apart from the body I do not know, but God knows—was caught up to paradise. (2 Corinthians 12:2-4, NIV)

Consider the glimpse of the writer of Hebrews:

> By faith Abraham, when called to go to a place he would later receive as his inheritance, obeyed and went, even though he

did not know where he was going. By faith he made his home in the promised land like a stranger in a foreign country; he lived in tents, as did Isaac and Jacob, who were heirs with him of the same promise. For he was looking forward to the city with foundations, whose architect and builder is God. (Hebrews 11:8-10, NIV)

Rejoice at the glimpse of the apostle Peter:

But in keeping with his promise we are looking forward to a new heaven and a new earth, the home of righteousness. (2 Peter 3:13, NIV)

Finally comes John's all-powerful glimpse:

After this I looked, and there before me was a door standing open in heaven. (Revelation 4:1, NIV)

For now we must trust these vague infrequent glimpses. As yet we have no photographs of heaven. But we have seen these towers glinting through the mists of our poor reality.

The glimpse is real. And we are certain that when the mists of death are cleared away, the whole city will stand visible and proud. Our inheritance is as sure as morning. Why are we so reluctant to leave this dingy world? Things really are better further on.

> *I once scorned ev'ry fearful thought of death,*
> *When it was but the end of pulse and breath,*

The glimpse is real. And we are certain that when the mists of death are cleared away, the whole city will stand visible and proud.

But now my eyes have seen that past the pain
There is a world that's waiting to be claimed.
Earthmaker, Holy, let me now depart,
For living's such a temporary art.
And dying is but getting dressed for God,
Our graves are merely doorways cut in sod.

—Calvin Miller, *Symphony in Sand*

THE THOUGHT OF GOD
Nagata

For I leave
this earth
To enter Heaven,
All things else
forgot,
All
disappointment
wiped away.

To me
The thought of God
Is this—

The first step
In my daily life.
Of all importance,
For I leave this earth
To enter Heaven,
All things else forgot,
All disappointment wiped away.

Unworthy though I am,
The thought of God
Is this—
Deep prayer
That is a well of shining hope,
And strength, and happiness.

It is a time when bounteous manna falls;
A time I learn the mysteries of the Word;
A time I breathe the breath of life,
And bathe my soul in God.

It is a time
When I see Heaven as my home;
The time I meet the Risen Christ!

20

A LETTER TO ADELAIDE

George MacDonald
from "Letters," The Heart of George MacDonald

Bordighera
8 February 1890

My dear Adelaide,

Let my heart come near to yours, and talk a little bit to it. If you are not able to listen, you can easily say to my messenger, "Wait till I can hear you."

We are all just children in our Father's nursery. Some of us are taken before others away from it, and we are left without our play-mates. But we know the Father has them, and though we must miss them constantly, we must remember that we shall be sent for by and by, and must by patient waiting be ready to go. You know all this as well as I do, but let us think it together.

What is all this life but a waiting? You who have suffered so much, must know that better than most! For myself, I have never been content with this world as a place to live in. I mean it has always, more and less, had the feel of a foreign land. The feeling has not been caused by much suffering, neither by any sense of outside failure. No doubt the world has been less satisfactory because of my own evil and great lack; but allowing for all that, there remains a something that indicates that it was never intended to be our home, and we were never intended to feel at home in it.

We must not then be unhappy when one of us goes to make the others happier who have gone before, and were waiting for them, and are now waiting for us to join them! The very notion of heaven is to have all we love with us, and God is just carrying out that notion for

The gates of heaven are so easily found when we are little, and they are always standing open to let children wander in.

—Sir James Matthew Barrie

us, by gentle recurrent removals as we are ready to go. It seems so commonplace when said to a sore heart—missing heart—but surely what you and anyone like you, and in such sorrow, needs is to "have your pure mind stirred up by way of remembrance."

But God has a marvellous bliss, and yet a very homely one, waiting for us. Be sure it will run in the old grooves, but the grooves will be of gold and gems, not of iron and clay. I think we shall talk of all the old times with the hearts of divinely glad little ones—and sometimes wonder that we made such a work about certain things. We shall have everything, for the Father who loves us, and is himself, as Dante calls him, "the glad creator," will see that his dear little ones are happy indeed, and have all they want. It will be safe then to give us all we want, for we shall not forget him, or forget that he gives us EVERY-THING.

And then what a thing it will be to feel our bodies as free, as little held down and oppressed, as our better part! Of course the great joy of heaven will be the same as that of this world—to know God and to be what he is; but we shall know him so much better then, and know how foolish it was of us to be troubled about anything when HE was looking after everything! There will be no question whether life is worth living to those who know what life means.

Things are just as right as they could be, so far as God is concerned, for the making us capable of his own joy in life. The only thing amiss is that we put our hope in other things than God, and wish things that are not worth giving us, and which therefore he does not care to give us, and so we do not work along with him for what he wants us to be and thereby delay the success of his work with us. For there is nothing good but being one with him in every desire and hope and joy.

My heart says these things to your heart, dear Adelaide, because they are life to it—or rather he who makes them truth, and is the truth, is life to it. He is our elder brother, watching ever for our good. We know what it is to have brothers to love; what is it to have a brother to love perfectly because he is a perfect brother!

So you must love Beatrice more than ever, and more yet, and wait in strong expecting patience: she will be more lovely still by the time we see her again—though that cannot be very long. Day runs so swiftly after day, and our "salvation" is nearer that when we believed.

Affectionately the friend of so many of you

George MacDonald

*H*eaven often seems distant and unknown, but if he who made the road thither is our guide, we need not fear to lose the way.

—Henry van Dyke

HEAVEN: PROMISED AND CERTAIN

I never saw a Moor—
I never saw the Sea—
Yet know I how the Heather looks
And what a Billow be.

I never spoke with God,
Nor visited in Heaven—
Yet certain am I of the Spot
As if the Chart were given—

—Emily Dickinson, adapted

Praise be to the God and Father of our Lord Jesus Christ! In his great mercy he has given us new birth into a living hope through the resurrection of Jesus Christ from the dead, and into an inheritance that can never perish, spoil or fade—kept in heaven for you, who through faith are shielded by God's power until the coming of the salvation that is ready to be revealed in the last time.

—1 Peter 1:3-5 (NIV)

There is nothing in the world of which I feel so certain. I have no idea what it will be like, and I am glad that I have not, as I am sure it would be wrong. I do not want it for myself as mere continuance, but I want it for my understanding of life. And moreover "God is love" appears to me nonsense in view of the world he has made, if there is no other.

—William Temple

When anyone is united to Christ,
there is a new world;
the old order has gone,
and a new order has already begun.

—2 Corinthians 5:17 (NEB)

It is unreasonable (and in fact escapist) not to plan for a trip to Australia before you go, especially if it is a one-way trip. But the trip to heaven or hell is surer, longer, and more certainly one-way than a trip to Australia. For every earthly trip, you at least make some inquiries at the travel bureau. The Church claims to be the heavenly travel bureau as well as the ship, the Noah's ark, in which we go. Simply to ignore this claim as escapism is the sheerest escapism.

The escapism of worldliness is compounded by the fact that we are already embarked on our journey to the other world. As soon as we are born, we begin to die. This world is like a rocket ship; we are already launched into the beyond. Life is an escalator, and there is no way off except at the end. The only choice is between directions: up or down.

—Peter J. Kreeft, *Heaven*

Beloved, we are God's children now; what we will be has not yet been revealed. What we do know is this: when he is revealed, we will be like him, for we will see him as he is. And all who have this hope in him purify themselves, just as he is pure.

—1 John 3:2-3 (NRSV)

For we know that when this tent we live in now is taken down—when we die and leave these bodies—we will have wonderful new bodies in heaven, homes that will be ours forevermore, made for us by God himself, and not by human hands. How weary we grow of our present bodies. That is why we look forward eagerly to the day when we shall have heavenly bodies which we shall put on like new clothes. For we shall not be merely spirits without bodies. These earthly bodies make us groan and sigh, but we wouldn't like to think of dying and having no bodies at all. We want to slip into our new bodies so that these dying bodies will, as it were, be swallowed up by everlasting life. This is what God has prepared for us.

—2 Corinthians 5:1-5 (TLB)

We look forward eagerly to the day when we shall have heavenly bodies which we shall put on like new clothes.

THERE AND NOW

Rachel Landrum Crumble

Beauty finds new voice there. Not this heart-
breaking elegy of ululating song.
Here, where late summer leaves turn dead
green, there the painter dabs a touch of yellow
so that Spring becomes a way of life. There, too,

Regret turns like an arrow in mid-flight,
becomes joy exploding brilliant as fireworks
in the never-ending day.

Here, imperfection marks the trail to beauty,
just as sin, a night-sky, shows the brilliance
of grace, a full moon.

There that moon is but one in a galaxy of bright
planets, the first letter in a mysterious alphabet
whose lexicons cannot exhaust words of praise.

I prayed with my mother on the phone
days before her death. Later, in a dream,
we prattled like school chums
on the alpine peaks of Heaven, her now
violet eyes washed of their green envy.

The prayers of my ancestors
echo peace to me across the canyon
of eternity. When I am destitute of history,
of hope, I have only to lay down my head
and listen.

VISIONS OF HEAVEN

Throughout the whole circumference of the earth, a dead wall, very near and very thick, obstructs the view. Here and there, on a Sunday or another season of seriousness, a slit is left open in its side. Heaven might be seen through these slits, but the eye that is habitually set for earthly things cannot, during such momentary glimpses, adjust itself to higher things. Unless you pause and look steadfastly, you will see neither clouds nor sunshine through these openings, nor the distant sky. The soul has looked on the world so long, and the world's picture is so firmly fixed in its eye, that when the soul is turned for a moment toward heaven, it feels only a quiver of inarticulate light and retains no distinct impression of the things that are unseen and eternal.

—W. Arnot

I saw Eternity the other night,
Like a great *Ring* of pure and endless light,
  All calm, as it was bright,
And round beneath it, Time, in hours, days, years,
  Driv'n by the spheres,
Like a vast shadow mov'd, in which the world
  And all her train were hurl'd.

—Henry Vaughan

I have had a tremor of bliss, a wink of heaven, a whisper. . . .

—T. S. Eliot, *Murder in the Cathedral*

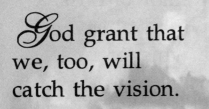

God grant that
we, too, will
catch the vision.

We are, I believe, given glimpses of heaven, and I have had a few. Walking down a dirt road on a shining summer day, I moved into a realm of beauty and depth that became indescribable once I had left it, but it gives me a hint that after I die I may say, "Oh, glory! What a thin way of living I have just left!"

—Madeleine L'Engle, *Penguins and Golden Calves,* adapted

Thank God for John who, many centuries ago, lifted his vision to high heaven and there saw the new Jerusalem in all of its magnificence. God grant that we, too, will catch the vision and move with unrelenting passion toward that city of complete life in which the length and the breadth and the height are equal. Only by reaching this city can we achieve our true essence.

—Martin Luther King, Jr., "Three Dimensions of a Complete Life"

What glorious vision breaks upon my eyes?
What heavenly prospect charms my raptured mind?
What wondrous beauties sudden round me rise?
  As if to dissipate my doubts designed.

What rapture, O my soul! the melody
Of seraph and of cherub strikes my ears,
Amid the tuneful choir I seem to be,
  And listen to the music of the spheres.

And does my God this place for me prepare?
And will these heavenly pleasures all be mine?
Shall I the glories of immortals share?
  O blest benificence of love divine!

—Thomas Cradock

Heaven itself will appear upon the horizon of our souls, like a morning light chafing away all our dark and gloomy doubtings before it. We shall not need then to light up our candles to seek for it in corners; no, it will display its own luster and brightness so before us, that we may see it in its own light, and ourselves the true possessors of it.

—John Smith, adapted

THE HIGHLANDS
Henry W. Frost

Oh, my heart is in the Highlan's
   O' the far and fair countree,
Where the King is waitin', waitin'
   For His ain, and e'en for me;
There He reigns in a' His glory,
   I shall see Him ane sweet day,
When He ca's me to the Highlan's
   Wi' Himself for aye to stay.

Ah, my heart was in the Lowlan's
   In the aulden, aulden time,
Midst the vapors and the shadows
   O' the lower, baser clime;
But the heavenly Man He sought me
   An' He deed for me straightwa';
Then He ga'ed back to the Highlan's
   An' He bore my heart awa'.

Oh, I love the bonnie Highlan's,
   Wi' its pure an' caller air,
Wi' its green fields an' its flowers
   An' its fragrance everywhere;
Ay, there's no place like the Highlan's
   For the soul frae sin set free;
'Tis a lan' o' wondrous beauty,
   'Tis the winsome lan' to me.

There's a palace in the Highlan's
    An' it glistens wi' the licht,
For the sun is ever shinin'
    An' there's never, never nicht,
An' there's music in the palace
    Sweeter far than a' the soun'
That e'er greets the list'nin' dwellers
    On the lower, Lowlan' groun'.

An' enthroned within the palace
    Is the King sae pure and fair,
Wi' His garments a' a-glist'nin'
    An' wi' shinin' snawy hair,
Wi' His face sae bricht, resplendent—
    'Bune the brichtness o' His croun—
That before Him a' the angels
    An' archangels fa' adoun.

Oh, my heart is in the Highlan's,
    Sae then dinna bid me stay,
For I canna but be hamesick
    For its gowden, blythesome day;
Ay, I'm wearyin' for its beauty,
    An' its licht that ne'er grows dim,
For the Ane wha's a' its glory
    An' a lastin' sicht o' Him!

There are
better things
ahead than any
we leave behind.

—C. S. Lewis

33

HOMESICK FOR HEAVEN

We have a homing instinct, a "home detector," and it doesn't ring for earth. That's why nearly every society in history except our own instinctively believes in life after death. Like the great mythic wanderers, like Ulysses and Aeneas, we have been trying to get home. Earth just doesn't smell like home. However good a road it is, however good a motel it is, however good a training camp it is, it is not home. Heaven is.

—Peter J. Kreeft, *Heaven*

Heaven

I live in light and love,
By God's grace given;
Yet is my hungry heart
Homesick for Heaven!

—Takamoto

There have been times when I think we do not desire heaven but more often I find myself wondering whether, in our heart of hearts, we have ever desired anything else.

—C. S. Lewis, *The Problem of Pain*

Begin, my tongue, some heavenly theme,
    And speak some boundless thing,
The mighty works or mightier name
    Of our eternal King.

Tell of his wondrous faithfulness,
    And sound his power abroad;
Sing the sweet promise of his grace
    And the performing God.

IIis every word of grace is strong,
    As that which built the skies;
The voice that rolls the stars along,
    Speaks all the promises.

O might I hear the heavenly tongue
    But whisper "Thou are mine,"
Those gentle words should raise my song
    To notes almost divine.

—Isaac Watts

The idea of heaven is the legacy of the most radical and most central hope. Heaven is the central and innermost significance of everything that man has ever hoped.

—Ladislaus Boros

Think of yourself just as a seed patiently wintering in the earth; waiting to come up a flower in the Gardener's good time, up into the *real* world, the real waking. I suppose that our whole present life, looked back on from there, will seem only a drowsy half-waking. We are here in the land of dreams. But cock-crow is coming. It is nearer now than when I began this letter.

—C. S. Lewis

Peace

My soul, there is a countrie
  Afar beyond the stars,
Where stands a winged sentrie
  All skilfull in the wars.
There, above noise and danger,
  Sweet peace sits crown'd with smiles,
And one born in a manger
  Commands the beauteous files.
He is thy gracious friend
  And (O my soul! awake)
Did in pure love descend,
  To die here for thy sake.
If thou canst get but thither,
  There growes the flowre of peace,
The rose that cannot wither,
  Thy fortresse, and thy ease.
Leave, then, thy foolish ranges;
  For none can thee secure
But One, who never changes,
  Thy God, thy Life, thy Cure.

—Henry Vaughan

If thou canst get but thither, There growes the flowre of peace

THE HEART OF THE MOUNTAIN

Mike Mason
from The Furniture of Heaven

> *The whole region was like a paradise that was right in front of the eyes, yet somehow could never be entered.*

In the days when the West was young, two brothers, Seth and Theo, settled on a homestead in a remote and rugged valley at the foot of a towering mountain. After several seasons of backbreaking toil, it became clear to them that the land was not as choice as they had first hoped. While on the surface the soil appeared rich and black, rain fell but stingily in those parts, and the growing season turned out to be unexpectedly short. Year after year the brothers picked rocks, cleared brush, and wrestled with the elements, yet still their crops came up sparse and stunted.

Like almost any spot on earth, the valley could often appear spectacularly beautiful. But the longer the brothers lived there, the more the wild glory of the place seemed to mock them with its inhospitableness. Winters were bitterly cold and stormy, and in summer the sun was a blister in the painfully bright sky. The whole region was like a paradise that was right in front of the eyes, yet somehow could never be entered. In addition to all the other hardships endured by the settlers, the mountain that loomed above their heads assumed a kind of hovering *presence,* almost as though it were haunted, or as though constantly threatening to come down upon their heads.

In spite of all this, the two brothers were a hard-working, good-living pair, who somehow managed to eke out a meager living from the stubborn soil. As poor as poor could be, yet they were able to wrest from their labors enough satisfaction to carry them through each day and into the next. And what more, realistically, could men ask out of life than that?

One frosty morning in early fall, Seth and Theo were surprised to wake up and find a goat standing in their yard. Although from time to time these creatures could be glimpsed high up on the mountain slopes, they were not known to frequent the valley, and domesticated goats were unheard of in those parts. However, as the brothers approached the animal she gave the impression of being perfectly tame, and allowed them to stroke her, to lead her into a corral, and even to milk her distended udders. Moreover, upon sampling this milk, they found it to be rich, creamy, abundant, and sweet as honey—in short, a product far superior to the insipid trickle of stuff that issued from their one cow. Where, they wondered, could such a fine and well-fed animal have come from?

For several days the brothers enjoyed this welcome gift from their mysterious guest. But one night, abruptly, just as inexplicably as the animal had appeared, she disappeared. Seth and Theo awoke in the morning to an empty corral, and though they searched the valley from one end to the other, not a trace of the wayfaring goat was to be found.

"Why didn't you let me tie her up as I suggested?" complained the elder Seth to his younger brother, as the bitterness of their loss set in. But sharp words and hard feelings could not bring the treasure back.

Instead, some days later, it happened that the goat returned of her own accord, reappearing just at a point when the brothers had given up all hope of ever seeing her again. This time they tethered her securely in the barn, and now the ambrosial milk tasted even more delicious to them than it had before.

Following a brief stay, however, once again the goat broke loose, and again no amount of searching could locate her. And so it came to pass that a kind of pattern began to develop, a haphazard though somewhat predictable pattern, in which every few days the animal would turn up out of the blue in the brothers' farmyard, and then just as suddenly she would vanish. Wherever it was she went off to, always on her return she would be healthy, sleek-coated, and laden with milk, as though having grazed her fill of sweet grasses in some lush and verdant pastureland. And while it was certainly true that the brothers had little enough of their own with which to feed the goat, still they made every effort to keep her from straying, yet all without success. For the creature seemed possessed of an infinite capacity for outwitting them.

One evening Theo, the younger brother, came up with a novel suggestion: "Instead of attempting to keep the goat here," he proposed, "why don't we try following her when she leaves? After all, wherever it is she disappears to, the land there must be much richer than our own, and it cannot be very far away."

Yet how were the men to know when the goat was about to depart? "No problem," said Theo. "We'll fasten one end of a long cord to our friend's tail, and the other end I'll tie around my own wrist. That way, as soon as I feel a tug I'll know that she's ready to leave, and then we can both drop whatever we're doing and follow her."

Although this seemed a simple enough plan, the actual implementation of it was not so easy. For it meant that during the next several days Theo had to accomplish all his chores around the farm with a long leash attached to his wrist. As awkward as this was at first, nevertheless he managed to complete his share of the work as usual, and was actually surprised at how accustomed he grew to the inconvenience.

Seth, however, found the situation an endless source of amusement and was constantly making snide comments such as: "It's a good thing my kid brother is tethered, or I'd be afraid he might run away on me!" Or: "So tell me, little brother, who's tied to who?"

One dark night, in the wee hours, Theo felt a gentle tug on his cord. Rising quickly from bed and throwing on some clothes, he hurried into the next room and shook his elder brother by the shoulder.

"Come, my brother, it's time!" he urged, as the tugs on the rope grew more insistent. "Come, our goat is leaving! It's the moment we've been waiting for!"

But it so happened that Seth had had a hard time of it that day, and had gone to sleep exhausted. In the middle of the night, in a warm bed, it seemed a foolish thing indeed to get up and go chasing off after some fickle, wandering goat.

"Go back to bed, my brother," he murmured sleepily. "Let's wait for another opportunity. The goat will come back."

When Theo shook Seth more vigorously, the latter responded angrily. "Don't you know what time it is?" he snarled. "Besides, only one of us needs to go. If you insist on running after this old nag, why not do it by yourself? Then you can return and tell me the way." And with that, Seth rolled over and went back to sleep.

Theo could wait no longer. Already he was being drawn irresistibly out of the room and down the stairs into the yard. It was a still, cold, incredibly black night, so dark that he could see no trace of the goat ahead of him, nor even make out his own feet. It was the sort of night in which one seemed to remember things one had never known, and with nothing but the pull on his wrist to guide him (almost as though this were no mere animal, but a person leading him gently yet urgently by the hand), the young man walked with strange assurance past the

It was the sort of night in which one seemed to remember things one had never known.

enormous shadow of the barn, through the unseen gate of the corral, and out into the frost-hard laneway.

Then after a while he felt his feet treading uphill, along a stony path. Sure enough, the goat must have headed in the direction of the mountain. The path would go on for a mile or so, Theo knew, and then it would come to an abrupt halt at the base of some sheer cliffs. And what was to happen then?

Up and up and over boulders and fallen trees they climbed, always rising, until finally they stood right beneath the towering shadow of the cliffs, where for the first time Theo caught a fleeting glimpse of the ghostly, white-bearded goat up ahead. She seemed, in fact, to be directly above him, walking straight up the vertical rock face! And then, all at once, without quite knowing how, the young man found himself following in her steps. He felt his feet gripping one tiny toehold, then another, and then sidling along the narrowest of rock ledges—narrow, almost, as a wire, narrow as the very cord tied around his wrist. And so up he went, straight up the precipice, poised and canny beyond any ken, his body melting like a shadow into the solid rock wall.

But this was only the first in a series of bewildering and impossible obstacles which, so long as Theo gave way to the sure tug of the rope against his flesh, he somehow managed to navigate with wondrous ease. Eventually, toward dawn, he heard a great sound of rushing water ahead, and then once more he caught sight of the goat, disappearing now behind the silver curtain of a high mountain waterfall. Following his guide through the cascade, and getting thoroughly drenched in the process, he was led next down a long dark tunnel full of twists and turns which finally emerged quite suddenly into an enormous open expanse, a sort of great subterranean cavern but without any walls, and dazzlingly illuminated. And there, in astonishment, Theo stopped short and rubbed his eyes.

Intuitively, he understood that this new interior world he had entered into was somehow the very heart of the mountain itself, the hollowed-out bosom of the rock! No sun was to be seen here, and yet the earth underfoot and everything in sight seemed to pour forth radiance and warmth, as though light and energy were emanating from within things. Overhead stretched not a stone ceiling, but a firmament of watersmooth silk, appearing deeper and more limitless (if such were possible) than the sky itself. Even the skin on the man's own hands shone with a lustrous color for which there was no earthly name.

The landscape here, for all its strangeness, had much the appearance of an alpine meadow, lushly carpeted with luminous emerald grasses and spangled everywhere with tiny star-like flowers. Nearby flowed a river, clear as new wine, and along its banks silver-leafed willows dense as haystacks seemed literally to drip with honey. In the distance flocks and herds grazed over gently rolling hills, and there were fields of thick ripe grain and orchards heavy with all kinds of fruit. As far as the eye could see, here was a land rich and fat and beautiful, overflowing with bounty.

How surprised and delighted the young man was to discover such a luxuriant garden paradise existing so very close to his own desolate homestead—indeed, just the skin of a mountain away! Without further delay he untied the cord from his wrist, knelt down beside the goat, and throwing his arms about her neck he wept in joy and gratitude, praising her again and again for having led him so strongly and surely to this heavenly place.

No sun was to be seen here, and yet the earth underfoot and everything in sight seemed to pour forth radiance and warmth, as though light and energy were emanating from within things.

43

Yet as full to the brim as his heart was just then, at the same time Theo could not help but feel a stab of remorse as he recalled his elder brother Seth, now left alone down below in the harsh barrenness of the valley. That very moment this lifetime partner of his would be going about the drudgery of their daily chores, almost certainly trying to accomplish the work of two, while entirely oblivious to the reality of this marvelous paradise so nearby.

At first Theo could think of nothing else but of returning to the valley at once to fetch his sibling. Long experience, however, had taught him that an elder brother does not listen to a younger brother when it comes to such things, and most probably would not even believe him. Besides, he knew that only the goat herself could guide a man along the tortuous path that led up the sheer rockface of the mountainside.

Accordingly, taking pen and paper from his pocket, Theo scribbled a brief note which read:

Dear Brother—

I am writing to you from a brand new land the glory of which is beyond description. Please believe me, this place is everything we have dreamed about, and it makes our little acreage look like a desert! You must join me here, and to do so you need only tether the goat to your hand, just as I did, and follow her up the mountain. Please come without delay.

Next Theo rolled up his note into a little tube and inserted it carefully into one of the goat's long ears. Though at present she was grazing contentedly, he knew that shortly she would return once again to the valley and stand in the front yard of the brothers' homestead, tacitly proffering her milk. Then Seth would come out of the house and welcome her, patting her on the head, whereupon the animal would wiggle her ears and the note would fall out. Although the skeptical elder brother might take a little time to mull matters over, soon enough he would be convinced, or at least intrigued. One thing would follow from another, and before long the pair would be reunited.

Satisfied then that he had done everything within his power, Theo went off happily to explore his abundant new paradise, from which all that was lacking was the presence of the one person closest to him in the world. And sure enough, after a few days of grazing in the lush meadows the goat did return as predicted down the mountainside, following the laneway back to the homestead, and finally standing placidly in the front yard, just as she had done so many times before.

By this stage, however, Seth had begun to grow angry over Theo's long absence, with a simmering anger that gave way gradually to fear, and a gnawing fear that spawned a yet more burning anger. What business had that kid brother of his running off after a stray animal? And abandoning him to do all the work of the farm alone? Indeed, if the rash fellow weren't dead by now, at the very least he'd be lying in a pile of rocks somewhere with a broken leg and would need to be rescued. And with a whole vast wilderness out there to comb through, how did the little fool ever expect to be found? Men were not made to go chasing after mountain goats!

Sullenly, smolderingly, out of the corner of an eye Seth stared and stared at the silent white creature standing quietly in the yard. Yet all day long he would not go near her, not even to collect her milk. For

Theo went off happily to explore his abundant new paradise, from which all that was lacking was the presence of the one person closest to him in the world.

in his heart he thought: "That goat is nothing but a troublemaker. Sure, she gives good milk. But she's also the bearer of ill fortune. She has led my brother astray, and now she dearly wants to entice me too. She would be the death of us both! But I won't give in. I'll not fall into her trap."

When, therefore, the man finally did approach the goat, it was not to pat her lovingly on the head. No. Nor did the animal wiggle her long ears, as the younger brother had expected. And neither did the all-important note come tumbling out onto the ground. No.

Instead, what happened was that just as dusk was settling over the valley and the sky was turning a smokey red, suddenly all the elder brother's suppressed anger and fear came boiling out, and he was gripped with an overwhelming passion. And creeping up behind the goat, with one decisive stroke, Seth split open her fine and gentle head with an axe.

And only then did his eyes fasten on the note, and only then did he recognize Theo's handwriting. But by the time he read the words, they were already soaked in blood.

MAGNIFICENT SPLENDOR

There is a glory which thou canst not see,
There is a music which thou canst not hear;
But if the spaces of Infinity
Unrolled themselves unto thine eye and ear,
Thou wouldst behold the crystal dome above
Lighted with living splendors, and the sound
Of their great voices uttering endless love
Would sink forever thro' the vast profound.

—Frederick Tennyson

What is your name? Is it a small darkened shadow? Is it just to make a living? Is it merely an opportunity to get the best seats as we ride this planet to its docking station? Is it merely an opportunity to gather life's perishables? If these crumbs are your goals and commitments, then your name is Swine.

But if you see the beckoning of the stars, if you hear the whisper of eternity, if you are willing to lose your life to find it, if you are willing to reflect the promise of the sunrise and the glory of the sunset—then get up; you are a fit candidate for eternity. Your name is written in the skies; your personality is part of the warp and woof of the very universe.

—Herman H. Watts, "What Is Your Name?"

No eye has seen, no ear has heard, no mind has conceived what God has prepared for those who love him.

—1 Corinthians 2:9 (NIV)

An old theologian once said, "Who chides a servant for taking away the first course of a feast when the second consists of far greater delicacies?" Who then can regret that this present world passes away when he sees that an eternal world of joy is coming? The first course is grace, but the second is glory, and that is as much better as the fruit is better than the blossom.

—Charles Haddon Spurgeon

At present we are on the outside of the world, the wrong side of the door. We discern the freshness and purity of morning, but they do not make us fresh and pure. We cannot mingle with the splendours we see. But all the leaves of the New Testament are rustling with the rumour that it will not always be so. Some day, God willing, we shall get *in*.

—C. S. Lewis, *Transposition and Other Essays*

For though we very truly hear that the kingdom of God will be filled with splendor, joy, happiness and glory, yet when these things are spoken of, they remain utterly remote from our perception, and, as it were, wrapped in obscurities, until that day comes when he will reveal to us his glory, that we may behold it face to face.

—John Calvin

Some have seen Paradise glimmering and wavering in the depths of loughs. Some have seen it rise up out of the sea and have heard the chime of its bells carried away on the wind. Others have looked out from the western cliffs and found it floating over the water like a bright shadow.

—Frederick Buechner, *Brendan*, adapted

The nearer I approach to the end of my pilgrimage, the clearer is the evidence of the divine origin of the Bible, the grandeur and sublimity of God's remedy for fallen man are more appreciated, and the future is illuminated with hope and joy.

—Samuel F. B. Morse

The Lord reigns as king, robed in majesty; royalty the Lord has for robe and girdle. He it was that founded the solid earth, to abide immovable. Firm stood thy throne ere ever the world began; from all eternity, thou art. Loud the rivers echo, Lord, loud the rivers echo, crashing down in flood. Magnificent the roar of eddying waters; magnificent the sea's rage; magnificent above these, the Lord reigns in heaven. How faithful, Lord, are thy promises! Holy is thy house, and must needs be holy until the end of time.

—Ronald Knox

How faithful, Lord, are thy promises!

O blessed mansion of the Heavenly City! O most clear day of Eternity, which the night may not darken, but the high Truth, that is God, illumineth and cleareth. Day always merry, always sure, and never changing its state into the contrary. Would to God that this day might once appear and shine upon us, and that these temporal things were at an end. This blessed day shineth to Saints in heaven with everlasting brightness and clarity, but to us pilgrims on earth it shineth not but afar off, as through a glass.

—Thomas à Kempis, *The Imitation of Christ*, translation by Richard Whitford

I WAIT IN PURPLE CONTEMPLATION

from "For Behold The Day Cometh"
Walter Wangerin, Jr.
adapted

I had a dream. It was a simple dream, more feeling than detail, but it seemed to last a long while.

Simply, a friend of mine was coming to see me, and I was excited by the prospect. I didn't know who the friend was. That didn't seem odd. I suppose I didn't occupy myself with the question Who. Just with the anticipation, and with the certainty that he would come.

As the time for his arrival drew nearer and nearer, my excitement increased. I felt more and more like a child, beaming with my pleasure, distracted from all other pursuits, thinking of this one thing only. I found that laughter fell from me as easy as rain. I wanted to stand on the porch and bellow to the neighborhood, My friend is coming! Joy became a sort of swelling in my chest, and all my flesh began to tingle.

Well, it was clear that I hadn't seen this friend for years. Even in the intensity of excitement, I didn't picture him to myself. Perhaps I didn't know what he looked like. Is that possible? Yet I had no doubt that he was dear to me, and I to him; that he satisfied the fathomless need in me; and that it was me in particular whom he chose to visit. I could scarcely stand the waiting.

Strangely, I think I expected to recognize him by his scent, by a certain smell I remembered, rich and steadfast, fleshly, warm, enveloping—like the strong declaration of a stallion's flank after galloping. It wasn't so much my eyes I strained, then, but my nostrils and the fullness of my mouth.

A wild kind of music attended my waiting. And the closer he came, the more exquisite grew this music—high violins rising higher by the

He satisfied the fathomless need in me.

51

sweetest, tightest, most piercing dissonance, reaching for, weeping for the final resolve of his appearing.

And when it had ascended to nearly impossible chords of wailing little notes; and when the familiar scent was a bounty around me; and when excitement had squeezed the breath from my lungs, I started to cry.

And he came.

Then I put my hands to my cheeks and cried and laughed at once.

He was looking directly at me, with mortal affection—and I grew so strong within his gaze. And I knew at once who he was. I was a perfect flame of the knowledge of his name. It was Jesus. He had come exactly as he said he would.

I cherish this dream and think of it often. I was a man full grown when I dreamt it.

The advent itself is ahead of me still, and that shall be no dream. It is a promise now; it will be the single most overwhelming event in the universe when it occurs. I confess that I tremble at the thought of the coming of One who shall dispopulate the graves and assemble the people and transfigure the whole of creation. But it is the grandeur, the uttermost awe of the thing that causes me to tremble. I am not afraid. And I will not hide. I wait in purple contemplation, peering through a clear patch in the stained-glass window. I watch, and I wait.

THE DWELLING PLACE OF GOD

God fell in love with us creatures of time, us passing gusts of wind, us passing guests, and invited us into the inner sanctum of the Master of the House forever—all of us, lock, stock, and barrel full of time. How dare we deny Him His heart's desire? It is our heart's desire too.

—Peter J. Kreeft, *Heaven*

Jesus said, "Let not your heart be troubled. You are trusting God, now trust in me. There are many homes up there where my Father lives, and I am going to prepare them for your coming. When everything is ready, then I will come and get you, so that you can always be with me where I am."

—John 14:1-3 (TLB), adapted

It was the Land of the Ever Young. There's no death there at all, you see. I glimpsed it for a moment only. It was floating over the water like a cloud. The beauty of it broke my heart, I think. I've scoured the seven seas for it ever since. I'm scouring them now.

—Frederick Buechner, *Brendan*

God has two dwelling places; one in heaven, and the other in a meek and thankful heart.

—Anonymous

Consider the immeasurable distance from us of what we know as God's dwelling place, the heavens; yet how near He is to us when we call upon Him.

—Midrash

Thou, O God, who art unchangeable. Thou art always and invariably to be found and always to be found unchanged. Whether in life or in death, no one journeys so far afield that thou art not to be found by him, that thou art not there, thou who art everywhere.

—Søren Aabye Kierkegaard

PRAYERS

Help us, O God, to glimpse the glory of life as it is lived with thee. We want to shape our daily needs according to thy will. Give us a vision of the eternal life. Save us from the doubts which would darken the end of life with what we know as death. Accept the dedication of what we are and have. Help us to understand the meaning of fellowship with thee, even for eternity. In Jesus' name. Amen.

—G. Ernest Thomas, *Daily Meditations on the Seven Last Words*

Lord, evermore give us this Resurrection, like your own in the body of your Transfiguration. Let us see and hear, and know, and be seen, and heard, and known, as you see, hear, and know. Give us glorified bodies through which to reveal the glorified thoughts which shall then inhabit us, when not only shall you reveal God, but each of us shall reveal you.

And for this, Lord Jesus, come—the child, the obedient God—that we may be one with you and with every man and woman whom you have made, in the Father.

—George MacDonald

O Lord—open up a window of heaven, And lean out far over the battlements of glory, And listen this morning.

—from "Listen, Lord—A Prayer," James Weldon Johnson

55

Glimpses of Splendor

Jesus, my joy in you is great
I want to praise you always.
When I was down and out
You stooped down to embrace me
Filling my soul with sweet, heavenly music.
Now you have silenced the ugly noise of sin within me
So I too can sing sweet spiritual songs,
Serenading your eternal love.
And as the melody of love springs forth from my soul
I realize that it is no more
Than the feeble echo of your perfect songs
With which you enchant the angels in heaven.

—Richard Rolle

A City Called Heaven

I am a poor pilgrim of sorrow,
I'm tossed in this wide world alone,
No hope have I for tomorrow,
I've started to make heaven my home.
Sometimes I am tossed and driven, Lord,
Sometimes I don't know where to roam,
I've heard of a city called heaven,
I've started to make it my home.

My mother has reached that pure glory,
My father's still walkin' in sin,
My brothers and sisters won't own me,
Because I am trying to get in.
Sometimes I am tossed and driven, Lord,
Sometimes I don't know where to roam,
I've heard of a city called heaven,
I've started to make it my home.

—Traditional

I've heard of a city called heaven, I've started to make it my home.

ACROSS THE CANYON OF

ETERNITY

THE ROAD TO GLORY

INTRODUCTION
Calvin Miller

We rose early for the climb. The stars were so close their light slid down the eroded peaks, washing the twisted pinnacles in eerie splendor.

> *The world is poor because*
> *her fortune is buried in the sky*
> *and all her treasure maps*
> *are the earth.*
>
> —Calvin Miller, *The Finale*

Stars are but the suns of distant solar systems. They are too distant to give us heat but close enough to give us light. Their light is remarkably steady. Once we leave the dimming smog of the cities, those distant suns move in close. We can see then the glaring finality of a universe we otherwise might doubt.

I recently stood with my wife on the south rim of the Grand Canyon. The evening shadows gathered to shout to silence the glaring panorama of the canyon's dying light. As we stood at the rail we watched an age old quarrel.

Each evening for millions of millennia the Colorado River and the desert have been at war. The desert has been losing. I never tire of watching that little silver strand of the Colorado, at its eternal business of lashing the eroding desert into humble peaks. Those ghostly defeated sentinels know they are losing. But at sunset they get mouthy, determined their struggle will not be quiet. These canyon peaks get sassy. They shout out their antagonisms in garish colors and snide shadows. Each night the lazy browns get gold. The angry golds scream their harsh carmines and arrogant reds. When their loud protests are done, the bolder colors quiet down to hoarse maroons. Finally, just before their exhausting fight is over, everything goes purple.

That night we watched as the purple mountains buried the Colorado in darkness. Then far across the canyon we watched as a blue-white mercury light winked on. It lay in the far away purple junipers like a misplaced star on the North Rim. That light was as clear as any of the stars that soon began to blink on in the upper skies. It was 28 miles away on the North Rim, but it seemed even further. We were planning in the morning to take a bus ride of 250 miles around to the North Rim so we could hike down "through" the canyon and back to the very place we had parked our car on the South Rim.

It would be a beautiful, but long and tiring hike.

Still, I was undaunted. "See that light?" I asked my wife. "That little star on the North Rim? Well, that's where we're going to be in the morning. And we're going to walk all the way back to this very spot."

"It seems so far," she said. "Besides, we're getting too—shall I say it—old for all this kind of stuff." Her protest poured ice-water on my enthusiasm.

"Listen," I reproved, "we are not too old. This will be the odyssey of a lifetime. See this beautiful world—it is ours. We are *not* that old. What do you want—to play the easy tourist and miss this wonderful trip? Do you want us to spend our entire vacation drinking diet colas and feeding corn-nuts to rabid chipmunks on the South Rim?"

My rebuke finished our conversation.

She repented of her near refusal.

After a night of sleep we rose early to meet the van that would take us to the North Rim. Once there we began our wonderful walk to "Phantom Ranch" where we would spend the night, before we began to climb out. We rose early for the climb. The stars were so close their light slid down the eroded peaks, washing the twisted pinnacles in eerie splendor. On we climbed toward the South Rim. Yes, our legs were screaming in their objection to our starry climb. But the beauty of the stars cheered us. Some of those distant suns gathered themselves into the peeping Orion who watched our night climb.

Yes, we are older. One day our systems will be too frail to challenge starlit trails. Then we will wait to test the metaphors of the final climb. But for now our vigor equaled our exhilaration. At last we reached the rim. We were exhausted. We went to our hotel and rested. Then as evening drew near, we walked back out on the South Rim. We once more studied the darkening canyon from the heights. Had we really walked that tedious course? Had we really been in the dark world below us? Had we passed those ebony mountains in the darkness? Had we tamed their terrors with our weak certainties?

Just as we asked all the questions about our sojourn, the same light blinked on once more. The North Rim. The same familiar blue-white star snuggled into the same purple shadows.

"Look!" Barbara cried.

Then she smiled and asked, "Were we really over there? Have we come this far?"

Our eyes fell from the starlight to the dark shadows. Emily Dickinson's odd prophecy surfaced:

> I never saw a moor,
> I never saw the sea;
> Yet know I how the heather looks,
> And what a wave must be.
>
> I never spoke with God,
> Nor visited in heaven;

Yet certain am I of the spot
As if the chart were given.

We knew the truth now. Canyon travel is possible by starlight. And as I looked at the star on the rim I realized Jesus once left heaven. He traversed the canyon depths to earth. He crossed the void of death. He accomplished his redeeming work. Best of all, he made it clear that we too can cross the void. And here and there we can see it dimly in early haze. The very sight gives us confidence to journey on. Jesus crossed it. So can we.

Do the shadows seem dark?

Does the gulf seem wide?

It is but a little distance.

But no metaphor quite tells it all.

Never will any single allegory give us peace.

Often we are troubled by our coming journey into foreverness. Why? We know the journey we made together by starlight, we must one day make alone. One of us must one day stand at the bedside of the other. One of us must give the final counsel: "My darling, watch the rim star. I must kiss you to your journey. But do not tremble at the shadows. For as we part, I, the reluctant sojourner, now place your hand in the wounded hand of him who made the journey first, and guarantees your passage."

The canyon will be conquered once again. The rim star will appear. This distant flaming sun will guide us home. And there the first of us to reach the glorious rim will gaze above the night-lined chasm and smile above the crossing,

"Have we really come this far?"

Do the shadows seem dark? Does the gulf seem wide? It is but a little distance.

The promise!
It floats around us even now.
It swims this sand in maddening intrigue
With rapture as could cleanse a world's fatigue.
Earthmaker lives! His century has come.
There shall be love enough to strike us dumb.

—Calvin Miller, *A Symphony in Sand*

THE ENTRANCE TO THE GREATER WORLD

Every moment the voice of Love is coming from left and right,
We are bound for heaven: who has a mind to sight-seeing?
We have been in heaven, we have been friends of the angels;
Thither, Sire, let us return, for that is our country.

—Jalal Al-din Ar-rumi

Ain't-a That Good News?

I got a crown up in-a the Kingdom, ain't-a that good news?
I got a crown up in-a the Kingdom, ain't-a that good news?

I'm a-goin' to lay down this world,
Goin' to shoulder up my cross,
Goin' to take it home to my Jesus, ain't-a that good news?

—Traditional

There is no reaching heaven except by traveling the road that leads there.

—Anonymous

Reflection

I used to think—
Loving life so greatly—
That to die would be
Like leaving a party
Before the end.

Now I know that the party
Is really happening
Somewhere else;
That the light and the music—
Escaping in snatches
To make the pulse beat
And the tempo quicken—
Come from a long way
Away.

And I know too
That when I get there
The music will never
End.

—Evangeline Paterson

Look yonder at the cross! When life was ebbing away, Christ dismissed his pain-wracked body. His interest and concern were with the part of his being which in the moment of death would be released from the body. His spirit belonged to God, and heaven was his natural home.

We bow in silence before the miracle of Calvary. Our lives are different when we turn away from the scene. The focus of life is changed. The Cross enables us to see eternity at the end of our earthly road.

—G. Ernest Thomas, *Daily Meditations on the Seven Last Words*

What will it be, when they escape from the cramping ways of time and find themselves in the infinite? For the entrance of the greater world is wide and sure, and they who see the straitness and the painfulness from which they have been delivered must wonder exceedingly as they are received into those large rooms with joy and immortality.

—Amy Carmichael, *Mimosa*

For the entrance of the greater world is wide and sure . . .

Heaven is the place of victory and triumph. This is the battlefield; there is the triumphal procession. This is the land of the sword and the spear; that is the land of the wreath and the crown. Oh, what a thrill of joy will shoot through the hearts of all the blessed when their conquests will be made complete in heaven; when death itself, the last of foes, shall be slain, and Satan dragged as captive at the chariot wheels of Christ!

—Dwight L. Moody, *Heaven*

"Heavenly places in Christ." That is where God raises us. We do not get there by climbing, by aspiring, by struggling, by consecration, or by vows; God lifts us right straight up out of sin, inability and weakness, lust and disobedience, wrath and self-seeking—lifts us right up out of all this, "up, up to the whiter than snow shine," to the heavenly places where Jesus Christ lived when he was on earth, and where He lives to this hour in the fullness of the plenitude of His power. May God never relieve us from the wonder of it.

—Oswald Chambers

Not even the most learned philosopher or theologian knows what it is going to be like. But there is one thing which the simplest Christian knows—it is going to be all right. Somewhere, somewhen, somehow we who are worshiping God here will wake up to see Him as He is, and face to face. No doubt it will all be utterly different from anything we have ever imagined or thought about it. No doubt God Himself will be unimaginably different from all our present conceptions of Him. But He will be unimaginably different only because He will be unimaginably better. The only thing we do certainly know is that our highest hopes will be more than fulfilled, and our deepest longings more than gratified.

—John Baillie

We are alone when we enter the world, but when we leave it we shall feel the abiding presence of the Lord. As death draws near and we dread the dark journey ahead, the Lord will assure us that our lives are precious in the sight of God. He will gently say, "Child, come home." Jesus has given His word that He will never leave us or forsake us, and his word is as firm as His character.

—Edward John Carnell

Somewhere, somewhen, somehow we who are worshiping God here will wake up to see Him as He is, and face to face.

*I'll praise my
Maker while I've
breath;
And when my
voice is lost in
death
Praise shall
employ my
nobler powers;
My days of
praise shall ne'er
be past,
While life and
thought and
being last,
Or immortality
endures.*

—John Wesley

MY HEAVEN IS TO PLEASE GOD

David Brainerd
As quoted by Jonathan Edwards in "Funeral Sermon for David Brainerd"

My heaven is to please God, to glorify him, to give all to him, and to be wholly devoted to his glory: That is the heaven I long for; that is my religion; that is my happiness; and always was, ever since I supposed I had any true religion.—I do not go to heaven to be advanced; but to give honor to God. It is no matter where I shall be stationed in heaven; whether I have a high or low seat there, but I go to love, and please, and glorify God. If I had a thousand souls, if they were worth anything, I would give them all to God: But I have nothing to give, when all is done. It is impossible for any rational creature to be happy without acting all for God; God himself could not make me happy in any other way.—I long to be in heaven, praising and glorifying God with the holy angels; all my desire is to glorify God.—My heart goes out to the burying place, it seems to me a desirable place: But O to glorify God! That is it! That is above all!—It is a great comfort to me to think that I have done a little for God in the world: It is but a very small matter; yet I have done a little; and I lament that I have not done more for him.—There is nothing in this world worth living for, but doing good, and finishing God's work; doing the work that Christ did. I see nothing else in the world that can yield any satisfaction, beside living to God, pleasing him, and doing his whole will.

THE THIRD DAY

Rachel Landrum Crumble

That November morning, we chased whirling leaves,
laughing
    She walked in forever Spring.
We caught autumn in our lungs, our warm breaths
gathering with clouds of birds blown South.
         She brightened
    with effortless song, clear as Craig Pond in August.

When the phone rang, we splintered, silent and separate:
my son to his baby dreams, my daughter to the long shadows
of a season turned cold; me, to the frightening slow-
motion tremors from the Pacific Coast, rocking my kitchen
floor through fiber optics.

    She became one with that water, diving into the perfect
    circle of the sun: whole, as if never broken, standing
    inexplicably up, when constellations rise to sing
    the Hallelujah Chorus.

The topaz and garnet leaves we gathered to cheer her
flat green San Diego autumn wither, unmailed on the mantel.

    Her spent body lies cold and tagged at the morgue,
    three days empty.

*W*hen for ever
from our sight
Pass the stars,
the day, the night,
Lord of Angels,
on our eyes
Let eternal
morning rise,
 And shadows
end.

—Mary A. Lathburn

GLORY'S TRIUMPH

When we are tempted by longings to have with us again those who have passed on, let us think of their eternal joy—"pleasures for evermore." So all the pain is on our side, all the joy on theirs. It helps to remember this. Their bonds are loosed. The more we love them, the more we shall rejoice in their joy. "If ye loved Me, ye would rejoice, because I said, I go to unto the Father." That does not mean that there is no sorrow. "Ye shall be sorrowful," our Lord Jesus said—He knew that well—but He went on to say, "your sorrow shall be turned into joy." Sorrow is not eternal. Joy is eternal. "Weeping may endure for a night [stay with us as a passing guest for a night], but joy cometh in the morning," and stays with us through the day—the long, long day of Eternity.

—Amy Carmichael, *Thou Givest . . . They Gather*

Far, far above all earthly things,
 Triumphantly you rode:
You soared to heaven on eagles' wings,
 And found, and talked with God.

—John Wesley

All the Way My Savior Leads Me

All the way my Savior leads me;
What have I to ask beside?
Can I doubt His tender mercy,
Who through life has been my guide?
Heavenly peace, divinest comfort,
Here by faith in Him to dwell!
For I know, whate'er befall me,
Jesus doeth all things well.

All the way my Saviour leads me,
Cheers each winding path I tread,
Gives me grace for every trial,
Feeds me with the living bread.
Though my weary steps may falter,
And my soul athirst may be,
Gushing from the Rock before me,
Lo! a spring of joy I see.

All the way my Saviour leads me;
Oh, the fullness of His love!
Perfect rest to me is promised
In my Father's house above.
When my spirit, clothed immortal,
Wings its flight to realms of day;
This my song thro' endless ages:
Jesus led me all the way.

—Fanny Jane Crosby

Sir Walter Scott told the story of the triumphant death of Ephraim Macbriar. Captured and condemned to death because of his faith, Macbriar was led through weeping crowds to his execution. "Farewell," he cried, "farewell, farewell! Farewell the world of all delights! Farewell sun, moon, and stars! Welcome God the Father! Welcome sweet Jesus Christ! Welcome blessed spirit! Welcome glory! Welcome eternal life! Welcome death!"

—G. Ernest Thomas, *Daily Meditations on the Seven Last Words*

Our valleys may be filled with foes and tears; but we can lift our eyes to the hills to see God and the angels, heaven's spectators, who support us according to God's infinite wisdom as they prepare our welcome home.

—Billy Graham

*W*elcome God the Father! Welcome sweet Jesus Christ! Welcome blessed spirit! Welcome glory!

Go Down Death—a Funeral Sermon

. . . Death didn't frighten Sister Caroline;
He looked to her like a welcome friend.
And she whispered to us: I'm going home,
And she smiled and closed her eyes.

And Death took her up like a baby,
And she lay in his icy arms,
But she didn't feel no chill.
And Death began to ride again—
Up beyond the evening star,
Out beyond the morning star,
Into the glittering light of glory,
On to the Great White Throne.

—James Weldon Johnson

ONE ETERNAL DAY
from "On Jordan's Stormy Banks I Stand"
Samuel Stennet

O the transporting, rapturous scene,
  That rises to my sight;
Sweet fields arrayed in living green,
  And rivers of delight!

O'er all those wide-extended plains
  Shines one eternal day;
There God the Son forever reigns,
  And scatters night away.

No chilling winds, or poisonous breath,
  Can reach that healthful shore;
Sickness and sorrow, pain and death,
  Are felt and feared no more.

When shall I reach that happy place,
  And be forever blest?
When shall I see my Father's face,
  And in his bosom rest?

Filled with delight, my raptured soul
  Would here no longer stay:
Though Jordan's waves around me roll,
  Fearless I'd launch away.

THE NORTH WIND

from At the Back of the North Wind
George MacDonald

Diamond Questions North Wind

My readers will not wonder that I did my very best to gain the friendship of Diamond. Nor did I find this at all difficult, the child was so ready to trust. Upon one subject alone was he reticent—the story of his relations with North Wind. I fancy he could not quite make up his mind what to think of them. At all events it was some little time before he trusted me with this, only then he told me everything. If I could not regard it all in exactly the same light as he did, I was, while guiltless of the least pretense, fully sympathetic, and he was satisfied without demanding of me any theory of difficult points involved. I let him see plainly enough, that whatever might be the explanation of the marvelous experience, I would have given much for a similar one myself.

On an evening soon after the thunderstorm, in a late twilight, with a half-moon high in the heavens, I came upon Diamond in the act of climbing by his ladder into the beech tree.

"What are you always going up there for, Diamond?" I heard Nanny ask, rather rudely, I thought.

"Sometimes for one thing, sometimes for another, Nanny," answered Diamond, looking skywards as he climbed.

"You'll break your neck someday," she said.

"I'm going up to look at the moon tonight," he added, without heeding her remark.

"You'll see the moon just as well down here," she returned.

"I don't think so."

"You'll be no nearer to her up there."

Whatever might be the explanation of the marvelous experience, I would have given much for a similar one myself.

77

"*D*reams ain't true."

"That one was true, Nanny. You know it was."

"Oh, yes, I shall! I must be nearer her, you know. I wish I could dream as pretty dreams about her as you can, Nanny."

"You silly! You never have done about that dream. I never dreamed but that one, and it was nonsense enough, I'm sure."

"It wasn't nonsense. It was a beautiful dream—and a funny one too, both in one."

"But what's the good of talking about it that way, when you know it was only a dream? Dreams ain't true."

"That one was true, Nanny. You know it was. Didn't you come to grief for doing what you were told not to? And isn't that true?"

"I can't get any sense into him," exclaimed Nanny, with an expression of mild despair. "Do you really believe, Diamond, that there's a house in the moon, with a beautiful lady, and a crooked old man and dusters in it?"

"If there isn't, there's something better," he answered, and vanished in the leaves over our heads.

I went into the house, where I visited often in the evenings. When I came out, there was a little wind blowing, very pleasant after the heat of the day, for though it was late summer now it was still hot. The treetops were swinging about in it. I took my way past the beech, and called up to see if Diamond was still in his nest in its rocking head.

"Are you there, Diamond?" I said.

"Yes, sir," came his clear voice in reply.

"Isn't it growing too dark for you to get down safely?"

"Oh, no, sir—if I take time to it. I know my way so well, and never let go with one hand till I've a good hold with the other."

"Do be careful," I insisted—foolishly, seeing the boy was as careful as he could be already.

"I'm coming," he returned. "I've got all the moon I want tonight."

I heard a rustling and a rustling drawing nearer and nearer. Three or four minutes elapsed, and he appeared at length creeping down his little ladder. I took him in my arms, and set him on the ground.

"Thank you, sir," he said. "That's the north wind blowing, isn't it, sir?"

"I can't tell," I answered. "It feels cool and kind, and I think it may be. But I can't be sure except it were stronger, for a gentle wind might turn any way amongst the trunks of the trees."

"I shall know when I get up to my own room," said Diamond. "I think I hear my mistress's bell. Good night, sir."

He ran to the house, and I went home.

His mistress had rung for him only to send him to bed, for she was very careful over him, and I dare say thought he was not looking well. When he reached his own room, he opened both his windows, one of which looked to the north and the other to the east, to find how the wind blew. It blew right in at the northern window. Diamond was very glad, for he thought perhaps North Wind herself would come now: a real north wind had never blown all the time since he left London. But, as she always came of herself, and never when he was looking for her, and indeed almost never when he was thinking of her, he shut the east window, and went to bed. Perhaps some of my readers may wonder that he could go to sleep with such an expectation; and, indeed, if I had not known him, I should have wondered at it myself; but it was one of his peculiarities, and seemed nothing strange in him. He was so full of quietness that he could go to sleep almost at any time, if he only composed himself and let the sleep come. This time he went fast asleep as usual.

His feet grew stronger, and his body lighter, until at length it seemed as if he were borne up on the air, and could almost fly.

But he woke in the dim blue night. The moon had vanished. He thought he had heard a knocking at his door.

"Somebody wants me," he said to himself, and jumping out of bed, ran to open it.

But there was no one there. He closed it again, and, the noise still continuing, found that another door was rattling. It belonged to a closet, he thought, but he had never been able to open it. The wind blowing in at the window must be shaking it. He would go and see if it was so.

The door now opened quite easily, but to his surprise, instead of a closet he found a long narrow room. The moon, which was sinking in the west, shone in at an open window at the further end. The room was low with a coved ceiling, and occupied the whole top of the house, immediately under the roof. It was quite empty. The yellow light of the half-moon streamed over the dark floor. He was so delighted at the discovery of the strange desolate moonlit place close to his own snug little room that he began to dance and skip about the floor. The wind came in through the door he had left open and blew about him as he danced, and he kept turning towards it that it might blow in his face. He kept picturing to himself the many places, lovely and desolate, the hillsides and farmyards and tree tops and meadows, over which it had blown on its way to the Mound. And as he danced he grew more and more delighted with the motion and the wind; his feet grew stronger, and his body lighter, until at length it seemed as if he were borne up on the air, and could almost fly. So strong did his feeling become that at last he began to doubt whether he was not in one of those precious dreams he had so often had, in which he floated about on the air at will. But something made him look up, and to his unspeakable delight, he found his uplifted hands lying in those of North Wind, who was dancing with him, round and round the long bare room, her hair now falling to the floor, now filling the arched ceiling, her eyes shining on him like thinking stars, and the sweetest of grand smiles playing breezily about her beautiful mouth. She was, as so often before, of the height of a rather tall lady. She did not stoop in order to dance with him, but held his hands high in hers. When he saw her, he gave one spring, and his arms were about her neck, and her arms holding him to her bosom. The same moment she swept with him through the open window in at which the moon was shining, made a circuit like a bird about to alight, and settled with him in his nest on the top of the great beech tree. There she placed him on her lap and began to hush him as if he were her own baby, and Diamond was so entirely happy that he did not care to speak a word. At length, however, he found that he was going to sleep, and that would be to lose so much, that, pleasant as it was, he could not consent.

"Please, dear North Wind," he said, "I am so happy that I'm afraid it's a dream. How am I to know that it's not a dream?"

"What does it matter?" returned North Wind.

"I should cry," said Diamond.

"But why should you cry? The dream, if it is a dream, is a pleasant one—is it not?"

"That's just why I want it to be true."

"Have you forgotten what you said to Nanny about her dream?"

"It's not for the dream itself—I mean, it's not for the pleasure of it," answered Diamond, "for I have that, whether it be a dream or not; it's for you, North Wind: I can't bear to find it a dream, because then

I should lose you. You would be nobody then, and I could not bear that. You ain't a dream, are you, dear North Wind? Do say *No*, else I shall cry, and come awake, and you'll be gone forever. I daren't dream about you once again if you ain't anybody."

"I'm either not a dream, or there's something better that's not a dream, Diamond," said North Wind, in a rather sorrowful tone, he thought.

"But it's not something better—it's you I want, North Wind," he persisted, already beginning to cry a little.

She made no answer, but rose with him in her arms and sailed away over the tree tops till they came to a meadow, where a flock of sheep was feeding.

"Do you remember what the song you were singing a week ago says about Bo Peep—how she lost her sheep, but got twice as many lambs?" asked North Wind, sitting down on the grass, and placing him in her lap as before.

"Oh yes, I do, well enough," answered Diamond; "but I never just quite liked that rhyme."

"Why not, child?"

"Because it seems to say one's as good as another, or two new ones are better than one that's lost. I've been thinking about it a great deal, and it seems to me that although any one sixpence is as good as any other sixpence, not twenty lambs would do instead of one sheep whose face you knew. Somehow, when once you've looked into anybody's eyes, right deep down into them, I mean, nobody will do for that one anymore. Nobody, ever so beautiful or so good, will make up for that one going out of sight. So you see, North Wind, I can't help being frightened to think that perhaps I am only dreaming, and you are nowhere at all. Do tell me that you are my own real beautiful North Wind."

Again she rose, and shot herself into the air, as if uneasy because she could not answer him; and Diamond lay quiet in her arms, waiting for what she would say. He tried to see up into her face, for he was dreadfully afraid she was not answering him because she could not say that she was not a dream; but she had let her hair fall all over her face so that he could not see it. This frightened him still more.

"Do speak, North Wind," he said at last.

"I never speak when I have nothing to say," she replied.

"Then I do think you must be a real North Wind, and no dream," said Diamond.

"But I'm looking for something to say all the time."

"But I don't want you to say what's hard to find. If you were to say one word to comfort me that wasn't true, then I should know you must be a dream, for a great beautiful lady like you could never tell a lie."

"But she mightn't know how to say what she had to say, so that a little boy like you would understand it," said North Wind. "Here, let us get down again, and I will try to tell you what I think. You mustn't suppose I am able to answer all your questions, though. There are a great many things I don't understand more than you do."

She descended on a grassy hillock, in the midst of a wild furzy common. There was a rabbit warren underneath, and some of the rabbits came out of their holes, in the moonlight, looking very sober and wise, just like patriarchs standing in their tent doors, and looking about them before going to bed. When they saw North Wind, instead of turning round and vanishing again with a thump of their heels, they cantered

"*You* mustn't suppose I am able to answer all your questions, though. There are a great many things I don't understand more than you do."

"*The* real country . . . is ever so much more beautiful than that. You shall see it one day—perhaps before very long."

slowly up to her and snuffed all about her with their long upper lips, which moved every way at once. That was their way of kissing her; and, as she talked to Diamond, she would every now and then stroke down their furry backs, or lift and play with their long ears. They would, Diamond thought, have leaped upon her lap, but that he was there already.

"I think," said she, after they had been sitting silent for a while, "that if I were only a dream, you would not have been able to love me so. You love me when you are not with me, don't you?"

"Indeed I do," answered Diamond, stroking her hand. "I see! I see! How could I be able to love you as I do if you weren't there at all, you know? Besides, I couldn't be able to dream anything half so beautiful out of my own head; or if I did, I couldn't love a fancy of my own like that, could I?"

"I think not. You might have loved me in a dream, dreamily, and forgotten me when you woke, I dare say, but not loved me like a real being as you love me. Even then, I don't think you could dream anything that hadn't something real like it somewhere. But you've seen me in many shapes, Diamond: you remember I was a wolf once—don't you?"

"Oh yes—a good wolf that frightened a naughty drunken nurse."

"Well, suppose I were to turn ugly, would you rather I weren't a dream then?"

"Yes; for I should know that you were beautiful inside all the same. You would love me, and I should love you all the same. I shouldn't like you to look ugly, you know. But I shouldn't believe it a bit."

"Not if you saw it?"

"No, not if I saw it ever so plain."

"There's my Diamond! I will tell you all I know about it then. I don't think I am just what you fancy me to be. I have to shape myself various ways to various people. But the heart of me is true. People call me by dreadful names, and think they know all about me. But they don't. Sometimes they call me Bad Fortune, sometimes Evil Chance, sometimes Ruin; and they have another name for me which they think the most dreadful of all."

"What is that?" asked Diamond, smiling up in her face.

"I won't tell you that name. Do you remember having to go through me to get into the country at my back?"

"Oh yes, I do. How cold you were, North Wind, and so white, all but your lovely eyes! My heart grew like a lump of ice, and then I forgot for a while."

"You were very near knowing what they call me then. Would you be afraid of me if you had to go through me again?"

"No. Why should I? Indeed I should be glad enough, if it was only to get another peep of the country at your back."

"You've never seen it yet."

"Haven't I, North Wind? Oh! I'm sorry! I thought I had. What did I see then?"

"Only a picture of it. The real country at my real back is ever so much more beautiful than that. You shall see it one day—perhaps before very long."

"Do they sing songs there?"

"Don't you remember the dream you had about the little boys that dug for the stars?"

"Yes, that I do. I thought you must have had something to do with that dream, it was so beautiful."

"Yes; I gave you that dream."

"Oh, thank you. Did you give Nanny her dream too—about the moon and the bees?"

"Yes. I was the lady that sat at the window of the moon."

"Oh, thank you. I was almost sure you had something to do with that, too. And did you tell Mr. Raymond the story about Princess Daylight?"

"I believe I had something to do with it. At all events he thought about it one night when he couldn't sleep. But I want to ask you whether you remember the song the boy angels sang in that dream of yours."

"No. I couldn't keep it, do what I would, and I did try."

"That was my fault."

"How could that be, North Wind?"

"Because I didn't know it properly myself, and so I couldn't teach it to you. I could only make a rough guess at something like what it would be, and so I wasn't able to make you dream it hard enough to remember it. Nor would I have done so if I could, for it was not correct. I made you dream pictures of it, though. But you will hear the very song yourself when you get to the back of—"

"My own dear North Wind," said Diamond, finishing the sentence for her, and kissing the arm that held him leaning against her.

"And now we've settled all this—for the time, at least," said North Wind.

"But I can't feel quite sure yet," said Diamond.

"You must wait a while for that. Meantime you may be hopeful, and content not to be quite sure. Come now, I will take you home again, for it won't do to tire you too much."

"Oh, no, no. I'm not the least tired," pleaded Diamond.

"It is better, though."

"Very well; if you wish it," yielded Diamond with a sigh.

"You are a dear good boy," said North Wind. "I will come for you again tomorrow night and take you out for a longer time. We shall make a little journey together, in fact. We shall start earlier; and as the moon will be later, we shall have a little moonlight all the way."

She rose, and swept over the meadow and the trees. In a few moments the Mound appeared below them. She sank a little, and floated in at the window of Diamond's room. There she laid him on his bed, covered him over, and in a moment he was lapped in a dreamless sleep.

Once More

The next night Diamond was seated by his open window, with his head on his hand, rather tired, but so eagerly waiting for the promised visit that he was afraid he could not sleep. But he started suddenly and found that he had been already asleep. He rose, and looking out of the window saw something white against his beech tree. It was North Wind. She was holding by one hand to a top branch. Her hair and her garments went floating away behind her over the tree, whose top was swaying about while the others were still.

"Are you ready, Diamond?" she asked.

"Yes," answered Diamond, "quite ready."

In a moment she was at the window, and her arms came in and took him. She sailed away so swiftly that he could at first mark nothing but the speed with which the clouds above and the dim earth below

"Are you ready, Diamond?" she asked.
"Yes," answered Diamond, "quite ready."

And the song of the brook came up into Diamond's ears, and grew and grew and changed with every turn. It seemed to Diamond to be singing the story of its life to him.

went rushing past. But soon he began to see that the sky was very lovely, with mottled clouds all about the moon, on which she threw faint colors like those of mother-of-pearl, or an opal. The night was warm, and in the lady's arms he did not feel the wind which down below was making waves in the ripe corn, and ripples on the rivers and lakes. At length they descended on the side of an open earthy hill, just where, from beneath a stone, a spring came bubbling out.

"I am going to take you along this little brook," said North Wind. "I am not wanted for anything else tonight, so I can give you a treat."

She stooped over the stream, and holding Diamond down close to the surface of it, glided along level with its flow as it ran down the hill. And the song of the brook came up into Diamond's ears, and grew and grew and changed with every turn. It seemed to Diamond to be singing the story of its life to him. And so it was. It began with a musical tinkle which changed to a babble and then to a gentle rushing. Sometimes its song would almost cease, and then break out again, tinkle, and babble, and rush all at once. At the bottom of the hill they came to a small river, into which the brook flowed with a muffled but merry sound. Along the surface of the river, darkly clear below them in the moonlight, they floated; now, where it widened out into a little lake, they would hover for a moment over a bed of water lilies, and watch them swing about, folded in sleep, as the water on which they leaned swayed in the presence of North Wind; and now they would watch the fishes asleep among the roots below. Sometimes she would hold Diamond over a deep hollow curving into the bank, that he might look far into the cool stillness. Sometimes she would leave the river and sweep across a clover field. The bees were all at home, and the clover was asleep. Then she would return and follow the river. It grew wider and wider as it went. Now the armies of wheat and of oats would hang over its rush from the opposite banks; now the willows would dip low branches in its still waters; and now it would lead them through stately trees and grassy banks into a lovely garden, where the roses and lilies were asleep, the tender flowers quite folded up, and only a few wide-awake and sending out their life in sweet strong odors. Wider and wider grew the stream, until they came upon boats lying along its banks, which rocked a little in the flutter of North Wind's garments. Then came houses on the banks, each standing in a lovely lawn, with grand trees; and in parts the river was so high that some of the grass and the roots of some of the trees were under water, and Diamond, as they glided through between the stems, could see the grass at the bottom of the water. Then they would leave the river and float about and over the houses, one after another—beautiful rich houses, which, like fine trees, had taken centuries to grow. There was scarcely a light to be seen, and not a movement to be heard. All the people in them lay fast asleep.

"What a lot of dreams they must be dreaming!" said Diamond.

"Yes," returned North Wind. "They can't surely all be lies—can they?"

"I should think it depends a little on who dreams them," suggested Diamond.

"Yes," said North Wind. "The people who think lies, and do lies, are very likely to dream lies. But the people who love what is true will surely now and then dream true things. But then something depends on whether the dreams are home-grown, or whether the seed of them is blown over somebody else's garden wall. Ah! There's someone awake in this house!"

They were floating past a window in which a light was burning. Diamond heard a moan, and looked up anxiously in North Wind's face.

"It's a lady," said North Wind. "She can't sleep for pain."

"Couldn't you do something for her?" said Diamond.

"No, I can't. But you could."

"What could I do?"

"Sing a little song to her."

"She wouldn't hear me."

"I will take you in, and then she will hear you."

"But that would be rude, wouldn't it? You can go where you please, of course, but I should have no business in her room."

"You may trust me, Diamond. I shall take as good care of the lady as of you. The window is open. Come."

By a shaded lamp, a lady was seated in a white wrapper, trying to read, but moaning every minute. North Wind floated behind her chair, set Diamond down, and told him to sing something. He was a little frightened, but he thought a while, and then sang—

The sun is gone down,
  And the moon's in the sky:
But the sun will come up,
  And the moon be laid by.

The flower is asleep
  But it is not dead,
When the morning shines,
  It will lift its head.

> "*It*'s a lady," said North Wind. "She can't sleep for pain."
>
> "Couldn't you do something for her?" said Diamond.
>
> "No, I can't. But you could."
>
> "What could I do?"
>
> "Sing a little song to her."

When winter comes,
　It will die—no, no;
It will only hide
　From the frost and the snow.

Sure is the summer,
　Sure is the sun;
The night and the winter
　Are shadows that run.

The lady never lifted her eyes from her book, or her head from her hand.

As soon as Diamond had finished, North Wind lifted him and carried him away.

"Didn't the lady hear me?" asked Diamond, when they were once more floating down the river.

"Oh, yes, she heard you," answered North Wind.

"Was she frightened then?"

"Oh, no."

"Why didn't she look to see who it was?"

"She didn't know you were there."

"How could she hear me then?"

"She didn't hear you with her ears."

"What did she hear me with?"

"With her heart."

"Where did she think the words came from?"

"She thought they came out of the book she was reading. She will search all through tomorrow to find them, and won't be able to understand it at all."

"Oh, what fun!" said Diamond. "What *will* she do?"

"I can tell you what she won't do: she'll never forget the meaning of them; and she'll never be able to remember the words of them."

"If she sees them in Mr. Raymond's book, it will puzzle her, won't it?"

"Yes, that it will. She will never be able to understand it."

"Until she gets to the back of the north wind," suggested Diamond.

"Until she gets to the back of the north wind," assented the lady.

"Oh!" cried Diamond. "I know now where we are. Oh, do let me go into the old garden, and into mother's room, and Diamond's stall. I wonder if the hole is at the back of my bed still. I should like to stay there all the rest of the night. It won't take you long to get me home from here, will it, North Wind?"

"No," she answered; "you shall stay as long as you like."

"Oh, how jolly!" cried Diamond, as North Wind sailed over the house with him, and set him down on the lawn at the back.

Diamond ran about the lawn for a while in the moonlight. He found part of it cut up into flower beds, and the little summerhouse with the colored glass and the great elm tree gone. He did not like this, and ran into the stable. There were no horses there at all. He ran upstairs. The rooms were empty. The only thing left that he cared about was the hole in the wall where his little bed had stood; and that was not enough to make him wish to stop. He ran down the stair again, and out upon the lawn. There he threw himself down and began to cry. It was all so dreary and lost!

"I thought I liked the place so much," said Diamond to himself, "but I find I don't care about it. I suppose it's only the people in it that make you like a place, and when they're gone, it's dead, and you don't care a bit about it. North Wind told me I might stop as long as I liked, and I've stopped longer already. North Wind!" he cried aloud, turning his face towards the sky.

The moon was under a cloud, and all was looking dull and dismal. A star shot from the sky, and fell in the grass beside him. The moment it lighted, there stood North Wind.

"Oh!" cried Diamond joyfully. "Were you the shooting star?"

"Yes, my child."

"Did you hear me call you then?"

"Yes."

"So high up as that?"

"Yes; I heard you quite well."

"Do take me home."

"Have you had enough of your old home already?"

"Yes, more than enough. It isn't a home at all now."

"I thought that would be it," said North Wind. "Everything, dreaming and all, has got a soul in it, or else it's worth nothing, and we don't care a bit about it. Some of our thoughts are worth nothing, because they've got no soul in them. The brain puts them into the mind, not the mind into the brain."

"But how can you know about that, North Wind? You haven't got a body."

"If I hadn't, you wouldn't know anything about me. No creature can know another without the help of a body. But I don't care to talk about that. It is time for you to go home."

So saying, North Wind lifted Diamond and bore him away.

A star shot from the sky, and fell in the grass beside him. The moment it lighted, there stood North Wind.

"*Could* it be all
dreaming, do
you think, sir?"
he asked
anxiously.

I did not see Diamond for a week or so after this, and then he told me what I have now told you. I should have been astonished at his being able even to report such conversations as he said he had had with North Wind, had I not known already that some children are profound in metaphysics. But a fear crosses me, lest, by telling so much about my friend, I should lead people to mistake him for one of those consequential, priggish little monsters, who are always trying to say clever things, and looking to see whether people appreciate them. When a child like that dies, instead of having a silly book written about him, he should be stuffed like one of those awful big-headed fishes you see in museums. But Diamond never troubled his head about what people thought of him. He never set up for knowing better than others. The wisest things he said came out when he wanted one to help him with some difficulty he was in. He was not even offended with Nanny and Jim for calling him silly. He supposed there was something in it, though he could not quite understand what. I suspect however that the other name they gave him, *God's Baby*, had some share in reconciling him to it.

Happily for me, I was as much interested in metaphysics as Diamond himself, and therefore, while he recounted his conversations with North Wind, I did not find myself at all in a strange sea, although certainly I could not always feel the bottom, being indeed convinced that the bottom was miles away.

"*Could* it be all dreaming, do you think, sir?" he asked anxiously.

"I daren't say, Diamond," I answered. "But at least there is one thing you may be sure of, that there is a still better love than that of the wonderful being you call North Wind. Even if she be a dream, the dream of such a beautiful creature could not come to you by chance."

"Yes, I know," returned Diamond. "I know."

Then he was silent, but, I confess, appeared more thoughtful than satisfied.

The next time I saw him, he looked paler than usual.

"Have you seen your friend again?" I asked him.

"Yes," he answered solemnly.

"Did she take you out with her?"

"No. She did not speak to me. I woke all at once, as I generally do when I am going to see her, and there she was against the door into the big room, sitting just as I saw her sit on her own doorstep, as white as snow, and her eyes as blue as the heart of an iceberg. She looked at me, but never moved or spoke."

"Were you afraid?" I asked.

"No. Why should I?" he answered. "I only felt a little cold."

"Did she stay long?"

"I don't know. I fell asleep again. I think I have been rather cold ever since though," he added with a smile.

I did not quite like this, but I said nothing.

Four days after, I called again at the Mound. The maid who opened the door looked grave, but I suspected nothing. When I reached the drawing room, I saw Mrs. Raymond had been crying.

"Haven't you heard?" she said, seeing my questioning looks.

"I've heard nothing," I answered.

"This morning we found our dear little Diamond lying on the floor of the big attic-room, just outside his own door—fast asleep, as we thought. But when we took him up, we did not think he was asleep. We saw that—"

Here the kind-hearted lady broke out crying afresh.

"May I go and see him?" I asked.

"Yes," she sobbed. "You know your way to the top of the tower."

I walked up the winding stair, and entered his room. A lovely figure, as white and almost as clear as alabaster, was lying on the bed. I saw at once how it was. They thought he was dead. I knew that he had gone to the back of the north wind.

PRAYERS

We thank thee, O God, for the gift of death, for the great silence that comes after the noise and strife of this world. Yet we ask, if a man die shall he live again? To this cry of ages, O Heavenly Father, Easter has answered again, that great festival to immortality. The earth was dead and lo! it lives again; the grass is struggling beneath our thoughtless feet, the flowers we wantonly pick and waste are blooming; the Christ was crucified and lo his spirit still strives with men. The valley of the shadow of death is dark and all of us here, young and old and bad and good, must yet face it silent and alone. Beyond, the How and What and Where of those many mansions, Thou hast not said, O God, but this we know: we shall in some wise live—not surely in body, in soul we trust, and certainly in the deeds we do now, the memories we leave, the lives we influence and the ideals in which we dream. Of such and all immortal life make us worthy, O God—Amen.

—W. E. B. Du Bois, *Prayers for Dark People*

O God, the protector of all that trust thee, without whom nothing is strong, nothing is holy; increase and multiply upon us thy mercy; that, thou being our ruler and guide, we may so pass through things temporal, that we finally lose not things eternal: grant this, O heavenly Father, for Jesus Christ's sake our Lord. Amen

—*The Book of Common Prayer* (1662)

"Do not be worried and upset," Jesus told them. "Believe in God, and believe also in me. There are many rooms in my Father's house, and I am going to prepare a place for you."

—John 14:1-2 (TEV)

It is said that the path which leads to you is narrow and rough, with steep cliffs on either side plunging down into dark valleys. Yet the path on which you have put me is a royal road, broad and smooth.

To come to thee is to come home from exile, to come to land out of the raging storm, to come to rest after long labour, to come to the goal of my desires and the summit of my wishes. But Lord, how can a stone rise, how can a lump of clay come away from the horrible pit? O raise me, draw me. Thy grace can do it. Send forth thy Holy Spirit to kindle sacred flames of love in my heart, and I will continue to rise until I leave life and time behind me, and indeed come away.

—Charles Haddon Spurgeon

O my Lord, how obvious it is that you are almighty! There is no need to understand the reasons for your commands. So long as we love and obey you, we can be certain that you will direct us on to the right path. And as we tread that path, we will know that it is your power and love that has put us there. It is said that the path which leads to you is narrow and rough, with steep cliffs on either side plunging down into dark valleys. Yet the path on which you have put me is a royal road, broad and smooth. It is safe for anyone who chooses to take it. And your Son holds the hand of all who walk on it. If we become tired or discouraged, we need only look up to see your smiling face in the distance, inviting us to share your joy.

—Teresa of Avila

You alone, Lord, know how those who seek to imitate you must sweat. The path to heaven is steep, hard and rough, demanding every ounce of strength. We who tread that path enjoy no rest. Yet we are happy to leave all earthly pleasures far below, because they are empty and dull. And, though we can only glimpse it far above us, the beauty of the summit inspires our hearts and strengthens our souls. What peace, what bliss, what rapture, what freedom is to be found on the mountain of eternal life.

—John Sergieff, translation by E. E. Goulaeff

Help us to hope that the seeming Shadow of this Death is to our human blindness but the exceeding brightness of a newer greater life.

—W. E. B. Du Bois, *Prayers for Dark People*

ENTERING THE FAIR

COUNTRY

THE ETERNAL KINGDOM

INTRODUCTION
Calvin Miller

> *The first sound sleep we ever get on earth*
> *We must be roused one realm away.*

—Calvin Miller, *The Finale*

Growing up in a part of Oklahoma which is very close to Kansas, I have often thought of Oz. In fact, I once went to southwest Kansas to show the children where *The Wizard of Oz* was written. Kansas is of the earth, and Kansans are busy people who live in Kansas and think about Kansas a lot. I once thought a lot about Kansas. But now I am older. Kansas intrigues me less and less. Now I think more of Oz than of Kansas.

Oz was off limits to news of a tornado, and tornadoes are frequent in Kansas. Tornadoes were also the disorienting, fearful, and commonplace storms of my childhood. I have stood at a distance and watched them hanging from blackened thunderheads. I have peered out through basement windows and watched them destroy the neighborhood around us. Discussing tornadoes can be safe if the tornadoes are remote. I've seen them at a great distance and wondered at them, uninvolved. I find as much fun in watching these distant tornadoes as I do in discussing heaven over tea. But when the siren sounds for my neighborhood, the theology of tornadoes ends. Then in utter frailty I must counter those 500-mile winds that have demolished my neighborhood.

Hebrews 12:1-2 seems to discuss those saints in heaven who look down on earth:

Therefore, since we are surrounded by such a great cloud of witnesses, let us throw off everything that hinders and the sin that so easily entangles, and let us run with perseverance the race marked out for us.

Let us fix our eyes on Jesus, the author and perfecter of our faith, who for the joy set before him endured the cross, scorning its shame, and sat down at the right hand of the throne of God. (Hebrews 12:1-2, NIV)

It is easier to live in Oz, says Hebrews, and look for Kansas, than to live in Kansas and search for Oz. In Kansas, everybody has a theory about Oz. Streets of gold it has—they say. A crystal sea, too. There is a throne with lightning. The all powerful one, forbids evil and crushes witches while munchkins dance on yellow brick roads.

I've ministered to hundreds of dying people across my thirty-five years as a pastor. I've stood at many black-draped lecterns and told the grieving all I knew of Oz. Once I waited with a dying friend and heard him say, "I'm crossing over, pastor. Be here as I cross." He crossed and closed his eyes and opened them in the world I so much wanted to know about. "Tell me . . . what's it like?" I wanted to say, but he left me on the bank and stepped into the mist. Like Arthur, enshrouded in fog, he left me, and Oz remained a mystery. What of the common report of all these near-death experiences? Was there a tunnel and a light? Were you embraced by the light? Is there a yellow brick road and a million joyous munchkins?

Then I remembered the tale of a physician, a medical student, who at a particular holiday season was on a train going home. He was suddenly seized upon by a violent coughing spell. The spasm became so intense he collapsed, unconscious. When the train stopped he was taken to a local hospital and pronounced dead. His lifeless body was covered with a sheet and was left to be picked up by a local mortuary.

A nurse, however, saw his limp hand move. He was given a series of emergency treatments and soon revived.

During that period when he was pronounced dead, the young medical student had one of those customary "light at the end of the tunnel" experiences. His "death experience" ended with a personal confrontation of Jesus Christ. Christ rebuked him for the intense interest he had spent on being a doctor and the little interest he showed in the things of God. Two things make his experience stand out from a thousand-and-one other "tunnel-and-light" experiences. First, this doctor dates the event as the beginning of his real affair with Christ. He insists that his life desire is to be united with the Savior he met in the room that night. Second, his death is still the only death of anyone still affixed by a death certificate on court-house records.

If such a course is to be believed, here and there some may return from Oz. In John 12 is the curious case of Martha of Bethany giving a dinner for Jesus. It was the least she could do for a man who had just raised her brother from the dead. But John says that a great many people had come out from Jerusalem (John 12:9) to see Lazarus who would, of course, have been there eating. There is something quite believable about this story. It is most curious to watch a formerly dead man eat. Many of these who had earlier come to his funeral were now watching him do just that.

Could Lazarus have been the celebrity that all but eclipsed the glory of his great Redeemer? Well, he was back from Oz and his return was the subject of much conversation. In John 11:35 when Jesus brought him back from the grave, he wept. There are as many speculations given to Jesus' tears as there are theologians. But Jesus may very well have wept because he felt grief in calling Lazarus back from the Emerald City.

Lazarus, however, has no description of its beauty as far as Scripture records. Perhaps this is because we can never speculate on Oz unless we are actually there. When Emerson lay dying, his friend, Parker Pillsbury said, "Ralph, you're about to cross over. What's it like over there." Emerson simply said, "One world at a time Parker, one world at a time."

Of this we may be sure: Dorothy comes back to Kansas with a kind of story we can never give up. Kansas, like France or Argentina, is in the world at hand, and a million suicide notes have convinced us that this world is cruel. We are "marching to Zion . . . that beautiful city of God" and by comparison, this city is to be ours.

> Then I saw a new heaven and a new earth, for the first heaven and the first earth had passed away, and there was no longer any sea. I saw the Holy City, the new Jerusalem, coming down out of heaven from God, prepared as a bride, beautifully dressed for her husband. And I heard a loud voice from the throne saying, "Now the dwelling of God is with men, and he will live with them. They will be his people, and God himself will be with them and be their God. He will wipe every tear from their eyes. There will be no more death, or mourning or crying or pain, for the old order of things has passed away. (Revelation 21:1-4, NIV)

> Then the angel showed me the river of the water of life, as clear as crystal, flowing from the throne of God and of the Lamb down the middle of the great street of the city. On each side of the river stood the tree of life, bearing twelve crops of fruit,

There will be no more death, or mourning or crying or pain.

yielding its fruit every month. And the leaves of the tree are for the healing of the nations (Rev. 22:1-2, NIV).

Naturally it would be cause for weeping to leave the city of no tears and return to live on a planet where crying is a life-sign.

In a mausoleum in Ft. Worth there is an ash-filled urn which reads, "I'd rather be here than in Lubbock." The woman whose remains it contains had obviously not been excited by my glimpse of Oz. And we cannot help but wonder if Jesus wept in Bethany because he knew the truth. The city from which he recalled Lazarus was so much better than the harsh Bethany where his sisters wished him to be. Bethany, where the harshness of life would, for Lazarus, at last culminate in his second funeral. Jesus wept (John 11:35). Of course, he did. It's a crying matter to take some one from Oz and plop them down in stormy Kansas.

And we cannot help but wonder about the fictional Dorothy, as she lived out her years in rural Kansas. Long after Toto was in the pet cemetery outside Dodge City, where was Dorothy? Did she not yearn for that long-lost land of song and citadels. Jesus made it clear: Once you've caught a glimpse of Oz, Kansas is never quite good enough again.

> *Light is never given*
> *While we fear the dark.*

> —Calvin Miller, *The Finale*

THE JUDGMENT DAY

James Weldon Johnson
adapted

Early one of these mornings,
God's a going to call for Gabriel,
That tall, bright angel, Gabriel;
And God's a-going to say to him: Gabriel,
Blow your silver trumpet,
And wake the living nations.

And Gabriel's going to ask him: Lord,
How loud must I blow it?
And God's a-going to tell him: Gabriel,
Blow it calm and easy.
Then putting one foot on the mountain top,
And the other in the middle of the sea,
Gabriel's going to stand and blow his horn,
To wake the living nations.

Then God's a-going to say to him: Gabriel,
Once more blow your silver trumpet,
And wake the nations underground.

And Gabriel's going to ask him: Lord,
How loud must I blow it?
And God's a-going to tell him: Gabriel,
Like seven peals of thunder.
Then the tall, bright angel, Gabriel,

God's a-going
to say to him:
Gabriel,
Blow your silver
trumpet,
And wake the
living nations.

107

Will put one foot on the battlements of heaven
And the other on the steps of hell,
And blow that silver trumpet
Till he shakes old hell's foundations. . . .

And the living and the dead in the twinkling of an eye
Will be caught up in the middle of the air,
Before God's judgment bar. . . .

And God will divide the sheep from the goats,
The one on the right, the other on the left.
And to them on the right God's a-going to say:
Enter into my kingdom.
And those who've come through great tribulations,
And washed their robes in the blood of the Lamb,
They will enter in—
Clothed in spotless white,
With starry crowns upon their heads,
And silver slippers on their feet,
And harps within their hands;—

And two by two they'll walk
Up and down the golden street,
Feasting on the milk and honey
Singing new songs of Zion
Chattering with the angels
All around the Great White Throne. . . .

And I hear a voice, crying, crying:
Time shall be no more!
Time shall be no more!
Time shall be no more!
And the sun will go out like a candle in the wind,
The moon will turn to dripping blood,
The stars will fall like cinders,
And the sea will burn like tar;
And the earth shall melt away and be dissolved,
And the sky will roll up like a scroll.
With a wave of his hand God will blot out time,
And start the wheel of eternity. . . .

With a wave of
his hand God
will blot out time,
And start the
wheel of
eternity. . . .

> *C*ertain words grow to mean Heaven to us. These are my Heaven-words: "We shall be like Him; for we shall see Him as He is."
>
> —Amy Carmichael, *Thou Givest . . . They Gather*

RECONCILED

Heaven will be the perfection we have always longed for. All the things that made earth unlovely and tragic will be absent in heaven. There will be no more night, no death, no disease, no sorrow, no tears, no ignorance, no disappointment, no war. It will be filled with health, vigor, virility, knowledge, happiness, worship, love and perfection.

—Billy Graham

But our commonwealth is in heaven, and from it we await a Savior, the Lord Jesus Christ, who will change our lowly body to be like his glorious body, by the power which enables him even to subject all things to himself.

—Philippians 3:20-21 (RSV)

He was supreme in the beginning and—leading the resurrection parade—he is supreme in the end. From beginning to end he's there, towering far above everything, everyone. So spacious is he, so roomy, that everything of God finds its proper place in him without crowding. Not only that, but all the broken and dislocated pieces of the universe—people and things, animals and atoms—get properly fixed and fit together in vibrant harmonies, all because of his death, his blood that poured down from the Cross.

—Colossians 1:17-20 (THE MESSAGE)

Shall we know one another in Heaven? Shall we love and remember? I do not think anyone need wonder about this or doubt for a single moment. We are never told we shall, because, I expect, it was not necessary to say anything about this which our own hearts tell us. We do not need words. For if we think for a minute, we know. Would you be yourself if you did not love and remember? . . . We are told that we shall be like our Lord Jesus. Surely this does not mean in holiness only, but in everything; and does not He know and love and remember? He would not be Himself if He did not, and we should not be ourselves if we did not.

—Amy Carmichael, *Thou Givest . . . They Gather*

As the stars differ in glory, not according to their merits, but according to God's gift in their creation: So the bodies of saints shall differ in glory, not according to their merits, but according to God's free gift in the resurrection.

—William Fulke, adapted

In the Kingdom of Heaven all is in all, all is one, and all is ours.

—Meister Eckhart

ABOVE ALL

from "A Letter of Saint Andrew the Dancer"
Howard McCord

Above all

    the waters

        beyond the firmament

breathe and move

        in the restless

    and toiling thrust of creation,
lifted and dazzling

        and all participate
        are of

    the silent peace of the white and motionless light
and the contextured grains of earth

        the salt and wet
            reality

of the sea, the open gates

    the dance.

INDESCRIBABLE GLORY

I can touch but lightly upon these heavenly joys. There is a depth, a mystery to all that pertains to the divine life, which I dare not try to describe; I could not if I would, I would not if I could. A sacredness enfolds it all that curious eyes should not look upon. Suffice it to say, that no joy we know on earth, however rare, however sacred, can be more than the faintest shadow of the joy we there find; no dreams of rapture, here unrealized, approach the bliss of one moment, even, in that divine world. No sorrow; no pain; no sickness; no death; no partings; no disappointments; no tears but those of joy; no broken hopes; no mislaid plans; no night, nor storm, nor shadows even; but light and joy and love and peace and rest forever and forever. "Amen," and again my heart says reverently, "Amen."

—Rebecca Ruter Springer, *My Dream of Heaven*

The new life opens fair;
Before thy feet the blessed journey lies
   Through homelands everywhere;
And heaven to thee is all a sweet surprise.

—Washington Gladden

All I know is, we'll all be surprised.

—Lois Belch

113

> "*I* have come home at last! This is my real country! I belong here! This is the land I have been looking for all my life."

It is as hard to explain how this sunlit land was different from the old Narnia, as it would be to tell you how the fruits of that country taste. Perhaps you will get some idea of it, if you think like this. You may have been in a room in which there was a window that looked out on a lovely bay of the sea or a green valley that wound away among mountains. And in the wall of that room opposite to the window there may have been a looking glass. And as you turned away from the window you suddenly caught sight of that sea or the valley, all over again, in the looking glass. And the sea in the mirror, or the valley in the mirror, were in one sense just the same as the real ones: yet at the same time they were somehow different—deeper, more wonderful, more like places in a story: in a story you have never heard but very much want to know. The difference between old Narnia and the new Narnia was like that. The new one was a deeper country: every rock and flower and blade of grass looked as if it meant more. I can't describe it any better than that: if you ever get there, you will know what I mean.

It was the unicorn who summed up what everyone was feeling. He stamped his right fore-hoof on the ground and neighed and then cried: "I have come home at last! This is my real country! I belong here! This is the land I have been looking for all my life."

—C. S. Lewis, *The Last Battle*

Perhaps
　　　　after death
the strange timelessness, matterlessness,
　　absolute differentness
　　　　　　of eternity
will be shot through
like a starry night
with islands of familiar and beautiful
joys.

—from "Star Light," Madeleine L'Engle

　　To pretend to describe the excellence, the greatness or duration of the happiness of heaven by the most artful composition of words would be but to darken and cloud it; to talk of raptures and ecstasies, joy and singing, is but to set forth very low shadows of the reality.

—Jonathan Edwards

Now at last they were beginning Chapter One of the Great Story, which no one on earth has read: which goes on for ever: in which every chapter is better than the one before.

What might this life be like?

Perhaps the only way we can conceive of the nature of heaven is by earthly analogies. What does not appear in our experience (yet) cannot be defined, only related to what *does* appear in our experience by analogy. For instance, a suburban house in Long Island is to a slum in Calcutta what a castle in Switzerland is to a suburban house on Long Island. Even if you never lived in a castle, you know something about it by this analogy.

The problem is that we do not have a proper proportion with heaven as we do with Switzerland. If Calcutta is 2, Long Island 6, and Switzerland 18, heaven is not 54 but infinity. We must factor in the principle of transformation. Thus a better analogy would be that heaven is to earth as the butterfly is to the caterpillar.

—Peter J. Kreeft and Ronald K. Tacelli

The things that began to happen after that were so great and beautiful that I cannot write them. And for us this is the end of all the stories, and we can most truly say that they all lived happily ever after. But for them it was only the beginning of the real story. All their life in this world and all their adventures in Narnia had only been the cover and the title page: now at last they were beginning Chapter One of the Great Story, which no one on earth has read: which goes on for ever: in which every chapter is better than the one before.

—C. S. Lewis, *The Last Battle*

Let us always remember that the end of the resurrection is eternal happiness, of whose excellence scarcely the minutest part can be described by all that human tongues can say. For though we are truly told that the kingdom of God will be full of light, and gladness, and felicity, and glory, yet the things meant by these words remain most remote from sense, and as it were involved in enigma, until the day arrive on which he will manifest his glory to us face to face.

—John Calvin

No need of sun or moon in that day
  Which never is followed by night,
Where Jesus' beauties display
  A pure and permanent light.

The Lamb is their light and their sun,
  And lo, by reflection they shine,
With Jesus ineffably one,
  And bright with effulgence divine.

—Charles Wesley

THE ECHOING SONG

from A Tale of Foreverland
Carolyn Nystrom

"THE TIME IS COME!"
"COME, COME!"

The cry was faint, first beginning high among the peaks of Piris and Satoris. But as the water tumbling from the slopes gained momentum and became a gurgling, rushing, jubilant torrent, so the cry echoed and bounced from peak to peak, then gained intensity and joy as it reached toward the lush valley below.

"Come, come!"

"The time is come!"

From the hollows and peaks and valleys and forests responded those who heard the call. Their feet fairly danced along the paths and through the meadows. Children skipped hand in hand. A teenage girl carried a young baby. The old traveled as swiftly as the young, for their age showed in wisdom of face not in feebleness of body. Their voices were joyous. Some who had traveled this path before led the way while others to whom it was new followed excitedly in their wake.

Soon a song began, a simple melody, perhaps started by a child. Others joined and the melody repeated itself first high and then low and then all tones in between. The tune became as convoluted as the sparkling stream, almost turning back upon itself, then reaching out in a new adventurous direction. Each member of the throng sang his own version yet blended perfectly with the rest. The song was one of praise but the words were heard by Him alone. Only the magic of the music

118

reached the ears of the singers, for even they could not bear to know the strength of their combined words.

Still the cry was heard reaching into the most hidden of fertile valleys:

"The time is come."

"Come, come!"

"The time is come!"

For I am about
to create new
heavens
   and a new earth;
the former things
shall not be
remembered
   or come to
   mind.
But be glad and
rejoice forever
   in what I am
   creating.

—Isaiah 65:17-18 (NRSV)

O ONE, O ONLY MANSION!

St. Bernard of Cluny

O one, O only mansion!
   O Paradise of joy!
Where tears are ever banished
   And smiles have no alloy;
Thy loveliness oppresses
   All human thought and heart
And none, O Peace, O Sion,
   Can sing thee as thou art.

With Jasper glow thy bulwarks,
   Thy streets with emeralds blaze
The sardius and the topaz
   Unite in thee their rays;
Thine ageless walls are bounded
   With amethyst unpriced;
The saints build up thy fabric,
   And the corner-stone is Christ.

OH! WHAT A BEAUTIFUL CITY

Oh! What a beautiful city,
Oh! What a beautiful city,
Oh! What a beautiful city,
Twelve gates-a to the city, Hallelu!

Three gates in-a de east,
Three gates in-a de west,
Three gates in-a de north,
And three gates in-a de south,
Making it twelve gates-a to de city-a, Hallelu!

Oh! What a beautiful city,
Oh! What a beautiful city,
Oh! What a beautiful city,
Twelve gates-a to the city, Hallelu!

My Lord built-a dat city,
Said it was just-a fo' square;
Wanted all-a you sinners
To meet Him in-a de air;
'Cause He built twelve gates-a to de city-a, Hallelu!

—Traditional

THE CITY OF GOD

Consider a beautiful, clear night, and reflect how delightful it is to behold the sky bespangled with all that multitude and variety of stars. Next, join this beautiful sight with that of a fine day, so that the brightness of the sun may not prevent the clear view of the stars or of the moon. Then say boldly that all this beauty put together is nothing when compared with the excellence of the great paradise. Oh how lovely, how desirable is this place! Oh, how precious is this city!

—St. Francis of Sales, translation by John K. Ryan

Then I saw a new heaven and a new earth; the first heaven and the first earth had disappeared now, and there was no longer any sea. I saw the holy city, and the new Jerusalem, coming down from God out of heaven, as beautiful as a bride all dressed for her husband. Then I heard a loud voice call from the throne, "You see this city? Here God lives among men. He will make his home among them; they shall be his people, and he will be their God; his name is God-with-them."

—Revelation 21:1-3 (JB)

The city of God descending from heaven to dwell on earth and the bride adorned for her husband communicate God's blessed presence with his people; he will be their eternal source of joy.

—Robert A. Peterson, *Hell on Trial*

Oh how lovely, how desirable is this place! Oh, how precious is this city!

And the streets of the city shall be full of boys and girls playing in its streets.

—Zechariah 8:5 (RSV)

There is not one mansion there; there are many. The gates of heaven are twelve in number. There are not only three gates on the north, but on the east three gates, and on the west three gates, and on the south three gates. From opposite standpoints of the Christian world, from different quarters of human life and character, through various expressions of their common faith and hope, through diverse modes of conversion, through different portions of the Holy Scripture will the weary travelers enter the Heavenly City and meet each other—"not without surprise"—on the shores of the same river of life.

—Dwight L. Moody, *Heaven*

I Want to Be Ready

I want to be ready,
I want to be ready,
I want to be ready
  to walk in Jerusalem just like John.

O John, O John, what do you say?
  Walk in Jerusalem just like John.
That I'll be there at the coming day,
  Walk in Jerusalem just like John.

John said the city was just foursquare
  Walk in Jerusalem just like John.
And he declared he'd meet me there,
  Walk in Jerusalem just like John.

—Traditional

AS JOHN THE APOSTLE FIRST SAW THAT SIGHT

unknown fourteenth-century poet
from Pearl
translation by David Gould

II, I

From that spot my spirit sprang up in space;
My body lay sleeping upon the grave,
But my soul was gone by God's grace
On a venture to where marvels live.
I know not where in the world it was,
But I know I alit where cliffs cleave,
And toward a forest I turned my face
Where precious stones shone bright and brave.
Their radiance might no man believe,
The gleaming glory that from them glanced:
For never were clothes that women weave
Of half so much magnificence.

II, 2

Those hillsides were magnificent
With cliffs of crystal bright and clear.
Tall groves of trees upon them stand
With bright blue trunks. With leaves as fair
As burnished silver the boughs are bent
That glitter when they shake and stir:
When gleams of sunlight upon them glint,
With shimmering sheen they shine so sheer.

When we rise again with glorious bodies, in the power of the Lord, these bodies will be white and resplendent as the snow, more brilliant than the sun, more transparent than crystal, and each one will have a special mark of honor and glory.

—St. Catherine of Siena

Strewing the ground like gravel there
Were precious pearls of orient;
The sunbeams seemed but dark and drear
Compared with such magnificence.

II, 5

Magnificent were those precious depths
With beauteous banks of beryl bright,
Where sweetly swirling the waters swept
With a murmuring sound of pure delight.
Bright stones stood in the waters deep
As if through a glass shone glimmering lights,
As stars still staring while mortals sleep
Glow in the welkin on winter nights;
For every pebble that came in sight
Seemed emerald or sapphire in opulence,
And all the fountain gleamed with light,
So glorious its magnificence.

XVII, 2

As John the apostle first saw that sight,
I beheld that city of great renown:
The new Jerusalem richly bedight,
As it was descended from heaven down.
The city was all red gold bright;
Clear and transparent as glass it shone,

And garnished with jewels sparkling with light.
Twelve were the pillars it was based upon,
With twelve foundations from gemstones hewn,
And every tier was a separate stone:
As he so clearly describes this town
In Apocalypse, the apostle John.

XVII, 3

As John these stones in scripture named,
From his description I knew them all.
Jasper was the foremost gem
That glittered green on the basement wall,
The lowest but not the least of them.
Sapphire the second in order fell;
The chalcedony all sublime
In the third tier shone clear and pale.
The fourth was the emerald, greenest of all;
The sardonyx was the fifth stone;
Ruby the sixth, as we hear him tell
In Apocalypse, the apostle John.

XVII, 4

To these John added the chrysolite,
The gem that stood on the foundation seventh.
The eighth was the beryl clear and white;
The topaz twin-hued formed the ninth.

127

On the tenth tier, chrysopase was bright;
The stately jacinth graced the eleventh,
And the amethyst, noblest in all men's sight
With purple and indigo adorned the twelfth.
The wall well founded on the base beneath
Of jasper, like gleaming glass it shone:
I recognized it as he set it forth
In the Apocalypse, the apostle John.

XVIII, 2

Of sun or moon they had no need,
For God himself was their lamp-light,
The Lamb their lantern, a sun indeed:
Through him the city shone all bright.
Through walls and rooms did my glance proceed,
For all was transparent and clear to sight.
The high throne of glory was there displayed
With the elders around it, all dressed in white,
As John the apostle described it aright,
And the high God himself was seated thereon.
A river ran out of the throne more bright
By far than either the sun or moon.

XVIII, 5

Under the moon so great a miracle
No heart of flesh could well endure

*The Lamb
their lantern, a
sun indeed:
Through him the
city shone all
bright.*

As when I gazed upon that city wall,
So rare and marvellous was its allure.
I stood as still as a dazed quail
In amazement at that dream unsure;
My limbs could feel neither rest nor toil,
So was I ravished with its radiance pure:
For l dare say with conviction sure,
Had a bodily man endured that boon,
Though all physicians searched for a cure,
His life would be forfeit under the moon.

XIX, 2

With great delight they together fare
On golden streets that gleam like glass.
A hundred thousand I believe there were;
Hard to know who had the happiest face,
And all of one pattern the garments they wore.
The Lamb in the forefront did proudly pace,
With seven horns of red gold clear;
Like precious pearls his clothing was.
As toward the throne they together pass,
Though thick the throng, none quarrel or fight,
But mild as maidens meek at mass,
So fared they forth with great delight.

XIX, 3

Delight that his arrival wrought
Was greater by far than tongue can tell:
Those elders, on finding the one they sought,
Grovelling at his feet they fell.
Myriads of angels together brought
There scattered incense of sweetest smell.
To the angels the elders a new song taught
To praise that jewel that they love so well.
That song could pierce through the earth to hell
That the legions of heaven for joy recite.
With his servants the worth of the Lamb to tell,
Indeed I experienced great delight.

THE CITY OF LIGHT
Revelation 21:11–22:5 (THE MESSAGE)

The City shimmered like a precious gem, light-filled, pulsing light. She had a wall majestic and high with twelve gates. At each gate stood an Angel, and on the gates were inscribed the names of the Twelve Tribes of the sons of Israel: three gates on the east, three gates on the north, three gates on the south, three gates on the west. The wall was set on twelve foundations, the names of the Twelve Apostles of the Lamb inscribed on them.

The Angel speaking with me had a gold measuring stick to measure the City, its gates, and its wall. The City was laid out in a perfect square. He measured the City with the measuring stick: twelve thousand stadia, its length, width, and height all equal. Using the standard measure, the Angel measured the thickness of its wall: 144 cubits. The wall was jasper, the color of Glory, and the City was pure gold, translucent as glass. The foundations of the City walls were garnished with every precious gem imaginable: the first foundation jasper, the second sapphire, the third agate, the fourth emerald, the fifth onyx, the sixth carnelian, the seventh chrysolite, the eighth beryl, the ninth topaz, the tenth chrysoprase, the eleventh jacinth, the twelfth amethyst. The twelve gates were twelve pearls, each gate a single pearl.

The main street of the City was pure gold, translucent as glass. But there was no sign of a Temple, for the Lord God—the Sovereign-Strong—and the Lamb are the Temple. The City doesn't need sun or moon for light. God's Glory is its light, the Lamb its lamp! The nations will walk in its light and earth's kings bring in their splendor. Its gates will never be shut by day, and there won't be any night. They'll bring the glory and honor of the nations into the City. Nothing dirty or defiled will get into the City, and no one who defiles or deceives.

The City shimmered like a precious gem, light-filled, pulsing light.

Only those whose names are written in the Lamb's Book of Life will get in.

Then the Angel showed me Water-of-Life River, crystal bright. It flowed from the Throne of God and the Lamb, right down the middle of the street. The Tree of Life was planted on each side of the River, producing twelve kinds of fruit, a ripe fruit each month. The leaves of the Tree are for healing the nations. Never again will anything be cursed. The Throne of God and of the Lamb is at the center. His servants will offer God service—worshiping, they'll look on his face, their foreheads mirroring God. Never again will there be any night. No one will need lamplight or sunlight. The shining of God, the Master, is all the light anyone needs. And they wil rule with him age after age after age.

ETERNAL GLORY

There is a glory which thou canst not see,
There is a music which thou canst not hear;
But if the spaces of Infinity
Unrolled themselves unto thine eye and ear,
Thou wouldst behold the crystal dome above
Lighted with living splendors, and the sound
Of their great voices uttering endless love
Would sink forever thro' the vast profound.

—Frederick Tennyson

How barren a thing is Arithmetic! (and yet Arithmetic will tell you how many single grains of sand will fill this hollow Vault to the firmament) How empty a thing is Rhetoric! (and yet Rhetoric will make absent and remote things present to your understanding) How weak a thing is Poetry! (and yet Poetry is a counterfeit Creation, and makes things that are not, as though they were) How infirm, how impotent are all assistances, if they be put to express this Eternity!

—John Donne, *Sermons*, adapted

The heavens declare the glory of God.

—Psalm 19:1 (NIV)

It is not said, "May the joy of the Lord enter into thee," but "Enter thou into the joy of thy Lord," which is proof that the joy will be greater than we can conceive. We shall enter into a great sea of divine and eternal joy, which will fill us within and without, and surround us on all sides.

—Robert Bellarmine

We shall enter into a great sea of divine and eternal joy, which will fill us within and without.

There is no need to be worried by facetious people who try to make the Christian hope of "heaven" ridiculous by saying they do not want "to spend eternity playing harps." The answer to such people is that if they cannot understand books written for grown-ups, they should not talk about them. All the scriptural imagery (harps, crowns, gold, etc.) is, of course, a merely symbolic attempt to express the inexpressible. Musical instruments are mentioned because for many people (not all) music is the thing known in the present life which most strongly suggests ecstasy and infinity. Crowns are mentioned to suggest the fact that those who are united with God in eternity share His splendour and power and joy. Gold is mentioned to suggest the timelessness of Heaven (gold does not rust) and the preciousness of it. People who take these symbols literally might as well think that when Christ told us to be like doves, He meant that we were to lay eggs.

—C. S. Lewis

There [in our future life in heaven in our resurrection bodies of glory] we shall rest and we shall see; we shall see and we shall love; we shall love and we shall praise. Behold what shall be in the end shall not end.

—Augustine of Hippo, translation by Peter Toon

Hearts on earth say in the course of a joyful experience,
"I don't want this ever to end." But it invariably does.
The hearts of those in heaven say,
"I want this to go on forever."
And it will. There can be
no better news
than this.

—J. I. Packer, *Concise Theology*

A PRAYER

Bring us, O Lord God, at our last awakening into the house and gate of heaven, to enter that gate and dwell in that house, where there shall be no darkness nor dazzling, but one equal light; no noise nor silence, but one equal music; no fears nor hopes, but one equal possession; no ends or beginnings, but one equal eternity; in the habitations of thy majesty and thy glory, world without end.

—John Donne

*H*ow lovely is
your dwelling
place,
O Lord Almighty!

—Psalm 84:1 (NIV)

THE SOUND OF STRONG

THUNDER

INFINITE PRAISES

I think I heard the bells of trumpets blare the thunder of heaven's reassurance. The first time I heard it was when I was but a child.

Calvin Miller

The plague has fled,
And death itself is dead.
The dawn of hope is here.
Awake, ten thousand galaxies!
Polaris, bow your head! And Vega! Betelgeuse!

* * *

His dying world was weeping in the night.
He would not let it languish without light!
You sluggish quasars cease your cosmic flight
And listen! Here is a symphony of worth.
Oh, you proud skies, kneel down and kiss the earth!

—Calvin Miller, *A Symphony in Sand*

In *Paradise Lost* the fallen prince, Lucifer, is asked what he most missed about the paradise he had lost. He is quick to reply, "the sound of trumpets in the morning." Milton must be right. Trumpets are the instruments of heaven. Their loud, strong voices cry out the presence of the city's unforsaking King. Violins may introduce a nocturne and harps may call forth spring, but only trumpets have the clear and certain voice to sound the approach of kings.

Who can remember the form of life we shared with others before our memories began. I had a brother, five years older than myself. We must have played for hours, but all of that is lost to me. My brother went one day with childhood friends to swim in a farm pond not far from where we lived. He never came home again. After the shock and numbness, a million questions came to us. Did his struggle to breathe overcome his reason with final terror? When his drowning struggle ended, did he meet the Christ who blessed the children?

I think I heard the bells of trumpets blare the thunder of heaven's reassurance. The first time I heard it was when I was but a child—a child so small that memory all but starts there. Have you visited that first place where the mind remembers anything? I have.

My ten-year old brother was gone. I was barely five years old when my mother lifted me above his casket for a final look.

"Not coming back," she said.

"Where is he that he can't come back?" I asked.

"Heaven."

"Is it far from Garfield county?"

"Not far." She smiled.

I heard them sing at the funeral. I can't remember what they sang, but it must have been the old hymn "Beulah Land." I remember my mother singing that hymn so often over the next few years.

Oh Beulah Land, sweet Beulah Land,
As on a mighty rock I stand,
I look away across the sea
Where mansions are prepared for me
And glimpse the heavenly glory shore,
My hope, my heav'n forevermore.

She sang it all the time. I don't know why she sang. Perhaps grief can't quit hurting until it starts singing. She'd often stop and listen when she'd finish singing. Maybe she heard the thunder of some distant place. Maybe not, but she seemed so oddly silent as she sang. She seemed to stop to listen, and then she'd listen and sing. But in her odd litany of song and silence, she made me wonder if we are not most like heaven when we're singing. I've wondered if my little brother, who wasn't too far away, wasn't hearing some kind of continual music. I suppose if praise is the unending thunder of heaven, it's because heaven is filled with people who did a lot of grieving before they got there. It was grief that taught them the music even as heaven perfected their words. And the thunder rolls and trumpets speak clear notes of glory when the praise becomes so majestic that words can't say it anymore.

That's why the beasts of the Apocalypse fall down and cry: "Holy, holy, holy is the Lord God Almighty, who was, and is, and is to come" (Rev. 4:8, NIV).

Nor can the elders stand. They too sing best with their faces to the ground.

> "You are worthy, our Lord and God,
> to receive glory and honor and power,
> for you created all things,
> and by your will they were created and have their being."
> (Rev. 4:11, NIV)

And the roar of praise thickens as all the angels in heaven join in the singing:

> "Worthy is the Lamb, who was slain,
> To receive power and wealth and wisdom and strength

and honor and glory and praise!" (Rev. 5:12, NIV)

The elders seated on their thrones before God; fell on their faces and sang:

> "We give thanks to you, Lord God Almighty
> the One who is and who was,
> because you have taken your great power
> and have begun to reign." (Rev. 11:17, NIV)

That's why Isaiah's seraphim fly and cry, as clear as gold trumpets: "Holy, holy, holy. . . . The whole earth is full of his glory" (Isaiah 6:3).

Who would not enter this city singing? Who would not welcome the chance to exalt this King of Glory? Who has not at quiet midnights heard the glorious distant thunder of unending praise? I heard it as a boy of five. I'm not sure I would have heard it if my mother had not assured me heaven wasn't far from Garfield county.

I've never found it hard to believe in heaven. I've felt the quadraphonic rumble of God's tremolo. I've heard the distant thunder of praise. When the thunder died and I was no longer sure I had really heard it, I could still hear my mother. Her husky alto voice sang and convinced me. She sang so purely I could imagine all the beasts and elders stopping to listen to her music.

> There's a land that is fairer than day
> And by grace we can see it afar;
> For the Father waits over the way
> to prepare us a dwelling place there.

I've never found it hard to believe in heaven. I've felt the quadraphonic rumble of God's tremolo. I've heard the distant thunder of praise . . .

> In the sweet by and by,
> We shall meet on that beautiful shore.
> In the sweet by and by,
> We shall meet on that beautiful shore.

When she finally died I knew she held again that little boy, whose small earthly remains, like her own, lie yet in Garfield County. They must have smiled and studied each other in a lingering embrace of joy. Then they must have joined the unending praise breaking in the air around them. And then who can say? Perhaps the child, with his decades of practice, might have taught his mother the better music.

> *All universal being has, this night,*
> *Broken forth in long-awaited rhapsody,*
> *A woman's song has spawned a symphony.*

—Calvin Miller, *A Symphony in Sand*

HEAVEN

George Herbert

O who will show me those delights on high?
       Echo.   I.
Thou, Echo? thou art mortal, all men know.
       Echo.   No.
Wert thou not born among the trees and leaves?
       Echo.   Leaves.
And are there any leaves that still abide?
       Echo.   Bide.
What leaves are they? impart the matter wholly
       Echo.   Holy.
Are holy leaves the echo then of bliss?
       Echo.   Yes.
Then tell me, what is that supreme delight?
       Echo.   Light.
Light to the mind: what shall the will enjoy?
       Echo.   Joy.
But are there cares and business with the pleasure?
       Echo.   Leisure.
Light, joy, and leisure; but shall they persever?
       Echo.   Ever.

O who will show me those delights on high?

WHAT WONDROUS LOVE IS THIS

early nineteenth-century folk hymn, adapted

What wondrous love is this, O my soul! O my soul!
What wondrous love is this that caused the Lord of bliss
To bear the dreadful curse for my soul.

When I was sinking down, sinking down, sinking down;
When I was sinking down, beneath God's righteous frown,
Christ laid aside his crown for my soul.

Ye wingèd seraphs, fly! Bear the news! Bear the news!
Ye wingèd seraphs fly, like comets through the sky,
Fill vast eternity with the news!

Come, friends of Zion's king, join the praise, join the praise,
Come, friends of Zion's king, with hearts and voices sing,
And strike each tuneful string in his praise!

Yes, when to that bright world we arise, we arise;
When to that world we go, free from all pain and woe,
We'll join the happy throng, and sing on.

TO THE GATE

John Bunyan
from The Pilgrim's Progress, *adapted*

And thus it was: I writing of the way
And race of saints in this our gospel-day,
Fell suddenly into an allegory
About the journey, and the way to Glory.

Come hither,
And lay my book, thy head and heart together.

Now I saw in my dream, that by this time the pilgrims were got over the Enchanted Ground, and entering into the country of Beulah, whose air was very sweet and pleasant, the way lying directly through it, they solaced themselves there for a season. Yea, here they heard continually the singing of birds, and saw every day the flowers appear in the earth. In this country the sun shineth night and day; wherefore this was beyond the Valley of the Shadow of Death, and also out of the reach of Giant Despair; neither could they from this place so much as see Doubting-Castle. Here they were within sight of the city they were going to: also here met them some of the inhabitants thereof. For in this land the Shining Ones commonly walked, because it was upon the borders of Heaven. In this land also the contract between the bride and the Bridegroom was renewed: Yea here, *as the Bridegroom rejoiceth over the bride, so did their God rejoice over them.* Here they had no want of corn and wine; for in this place they met with abundance of what they had sought for in all their pilgrimage. Here they heard voices from out of the City, loud voices, saying, *Say ye to the daughter of Zion, Behold thy salvation cometh, behold his reward is with him.* Here all the

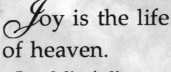

Joy is the life of heaven.

—Peter J. Kreeft, *Heaven*

inhabitants of the country called them, *The holy People, the redeemed of the Lord.*

Now as they walked in this land they had more rejoicing then in parts more remote from the kingdom to which they were bound; and drawing near to the City, they had yet a more perfect view thereof. It was builded of pearls and precious stones, also the street thereof was paved with gold, so that by reason of the natural glory of the City, and the reflection of the sunbeams upon it, Christian, with desire fell sick, Hopeful also had a fit or two of the same disease: wherefore here they lay by it a whole, crying out because of their pangs, *If you see my Beloved, tell him that I am sick of love.*

But being a little strengthened, and better able to bear their sickness, they walked on their way, and came yet nearer and nearer, where were orchards, vineyards, and gardens, and their gates opened into the Highway. Now as they came up to these places, behold the gardener stood in the way; to whom the pilgrims said, Whose goodly vineyards and gardens are these? He answered, They are the King's, and are planted here for his own delights, and also for the solace of pilgrims. So the gardener had them into the vineyards, and bid them refresh themselves with the dainties; he also shewed them there the King's walks and the arbors where he delighted to be: And here they tarried and slept.

I saw that when they awoke, they addressed themselves to go up to the City. But the reflection of the sun upon the City (for the City was pure gold) was so extremely glorious, that they could not, as yet, with open face behold it, but through an instrument made for that purpose. So I saw, that as they went on, there met them two men, in raiment that shone as the light.

These men asked the pilgrims whence they came? and they told them; they also asked them where they had lodg'd, what difficulties, dangers, what comforts and pleasures they had met in the way? and they told them. Then said the men that met them, You have but two difficulties more to meet with, and then you are in the City.

Christian then and his companion asked the men to go along with them, so they told them they would; but, said they, you must obtain it by your own faith. So I saw in my dream that they went on together till they came within sight of the Gate.

Now I further saw, that betwixt them and the Gate was a river, but there was no bridge to go over; the river was very deep; at the sight thereof of this river, the pilgrims were much astounded, but the men that went with them said, You must go through, or you cannot come at the Gate.

The pilgrims then began to inquire if there was no other way to the Gate; to which they answered, Yes; but there hath not any, save two, to wit, Enoch and Elijah, been permitted to tread that path, since the foundation of the world, nor shall, until the last trumpet shall sound. The pilgrims then, especially Christian, began to despond in his mind, and looked this way and that, but no way could be found by them, by which they might escape the river. Then they asked the men if the waters were all of a depth. They said no; yet they could not help them in that case; for said they, You shall find it deeper or shallower, as you believe in the King of that place.

Then they addressed themselves to the water; and entering, Christian began to sink, and crying out to his good friend Hopeful; he said, I sink in deep waters, the billows go over my head, all his waves go over me, *Selah.*

So I saw in my dream that they went on together till they came within sight of the Gate.

Then said the other, Be of good cheer, my brother, I feel the bottom, and it is good. Then said Christian, Ah my friend, the sorrows of death have compassed me about, I shall not see the land that flows with milk and honey. And with that, a great darkness and horror fell upon *Christian*, so that he could not see before him; also here he in great measure lost his senses, so that he could neither remember nor orderly talk of any of those sweet refreshments that he had met with in the way of his pilgrimage. But all the words that he spake still tended to discover that he had horror of mind, and hearty fears that he should die in the river, and never obtain entrance in at the Gate.

Here also, as they that stood by perceived, he was much in troublesome thoughts of the sins that he had committed, both since and before he began to be a pilgrim. 'Twas also observed that he was troubled with apparitions of hobgoblins and evil spirits; For ever and anon he would intimate so much by words. Hopeful therefore here had much ado to keep his brother's head above water, yea sometimes he would be quite gone down, and then ere a while he would rise up again half dead. Hopeful also would endeavour to comfort him, saying, Brother, I see the Gate, and men standing by it to receive us. But Christian would answer, 'Tis you, 'tis you they wait for, you have been Hopeful ever since I knew you: And so have you, said he to Christian. Ah Brother, said he, surely if I was right, he would now arise to help me; but for my sins he hath brought me into the snare, and hath left me. Then said Hopeful, My brother, you have quite forgot the text, where it's said of the wicked, *There is no band in their death, but their strength is firm, they are not troubled as other men, neither are they plagued like other men.* These troubles and distresses that you go through in these waters are no sign that God hath forsaken you, but are sent to try you, whether you will call to mind that which heretofore you have received of his goodness, and live upon him in your distresses.

Then I saw in my dream that Christian was as in a muse a while; to whom also Hopeful added this word, *Be of good cheer, Jesus Christ maketh thee whole:* And with that, Christian brake out with a loud voice, Oh I see him again! and he tells me, *When thou passest through the waters, I will be with thee, and through the rivers, they shall not overflow thee.* Then they both took courage, and the enemy was after that as still as a stone, until they were gone over. Christian therefore presently found ground to stand upon; and so it followed that the rest of the river was but shallow. Thus they got over. Now upon the bank of the river, on the other side, they saw the two shining men again, who there waited for them. Wherefore being come up out of the river, they saluted them, saying, *We are ministering spirits, sent forth to minister for those that shall be heirs of salvation.* Thus they went along towards the Gate. Now you must note that the City stood upon a mighty hill, but the pilgrims went up that hill *with ease,* because they had these two men to lead them up by the arms; also they had left their mortal garments behind them in the river: for though they went in with them, they came out without them. They therefore went up here with much agility and speed, though the foundation upon which the City was framed was higher than the clouds. They therefore went up through the regions of the air, sweetly talking as they went, being comforted, because they safely got over the river, and had such glorious companions to attend them.

The talk they had with the Shining Ones was about the glory of the place, who told them that the beauty and glory of it was inexpressible. There, said they, is the Mount Sion, the heavenly Jerusalem, the inumerable company of angels, and the spirits of just men

The foundation upon which the City was framed was higher than the clouds.

And when you come there, you shall have white robes given you, and your walk and talk shall be every day with the King, even all the days of eternity.

made perfect: You are going now, said they, to the Paradise of God, wherein you shall see the Tree of Life, and eat of the never-fading fruits thereof: And when you come there, you shall have white robes given you, and your walk and talk shall be every day with the King, even all the days of eternity. There you shall not see again such things as you saw when you were in the lower region upon the earth, to wit, sorrow, sickness, affliction, and death, *for the former things are passed away.*

The men then asked, What must we do in the holy place? To whom it was answered, You must there receive the comfort of all your toil, and have joy for all your sorrow; you must reap what you have sown, even the fruit of all your prayers and tears, and sufferings for the King by the way. There also you shall serve him continually with praise, with shouting and thanksgiving, whom you desired to serve in the world, though with much difficulty, because of the infirmity of your flesh. There your eyes shall be delighted with seeing, and your ears with hearing, the pleasant voice of the Mighty One.

Now while they were drawing near towards the Gate, behold a company of the heavenly host came out to meet them: To whom it was said, by the other two Shining Ones, These are the men that have loved our Lord, when they were in the world, and that have left all for his holy name, and hath sent us to fetch them, and we have brought them thus far on their desired journey; that they may go in and look their Redeemer in the face with joy. Then the heavenly host gave a great shout, saying, *Blessed are they that are called to the marriage supper of the Lamb.*

There came out also at this time to meet them, several of the King's trumpeters, clothed in white and shining raiment, who with melodious noises, and loud, made even the heavens to echo with their sound. These trumpeters saluted Christian and his fellow with ten thousand welcomes from the world: And this they did with shouting, and sound of trumpet.

This done, they compassed them round on every side; some went before, some behind, and some on the right hand, some on the left (as 'twere to guard them through the upper regions) continually sounding as they went, with melodious noise, in notes on high; so that the very sight was to them that could behold it, as if Heaven itself was come down to meet them.

And now were these two men, as 'twere, in Heaven, before they came at it; being swallowed up with the sight of angels, and with hearing of their melodious notes. Here also they had the City itself in view, and they thought they heard all the bells therein to ring, to welcome them thereto: but above all, the warm and joyful thoughts that they had about their own dwelling there, with such company, and that for ever and ever. Oh! by what toungue or pen can their glorious joy be expressed: and thus they came up to the Gate.

Now when they were come up to the Gate, there was written over it, in letters of gold, *Blessed are they that do his commandments, that they may have right to the Tree of Life; and may enter in through the Gates into the City.*

Now I saw in my dream, that these two men went in at the Gate; and lo, as they entered, they were transfigured, and they had raiment put on that shone like gold. There was also that met them with harps and crowns, and gave them to them; the harp to praise withal, and the crowns in token of honor: Then I heard in my dream, that all the bells in the City rang again for joy; and that it was said unto them, *Enter ye into the joy of your Lord.* I also heard the men themselves, that they sang with a loud voice, saying, *Blessing, honour, glory, and power, be to him that sitteth upon the throne, and to the Lamb for ever and ever.*

Now just as the gates were opened to let in the men, I looked in after them; and behold, the City shone like the sun, the streets also were paved with gold, and in them walked many with crowns on their heads, palms in their hands, and golden harps to sing praises withal.

There were also of them that had wings, and they answered one to another without intermission, saying, *Holy, holy, holy, is the Lord.*

GOD'S HOLY HABITATION

In the new order, which already exists in God's holy habitation there will be intimate fellowship between God and redeemed humanity with the absence of all that gives pain and sorrow and with the abundant presence of all that gives joy and life. Members of the new creation will actually see God and thus will be truly blessed.

—Peter Toon, *Heaven and Hell*

How lovely is thy dwelling place,
  O LORD of hosts!
My soul longs, yea, faints
  for the courts of the Lord;
my heart and flesh sing for joy
  to the living God.
Even the sparrow finds a home,
  and the swallow a nest for herself,
  where she may lay her young,
at thy altars, O LORD of hosts,
  my King and my God.
Blessed are those who dwell in thy house,
  ever singing thy praise!

—Psalm 84:1-4 (RSV)

I am the high and holy God, who lives forever. I live in a high and holy place.

—Isaiah 57:15 (TEV)

He is infinite, omnipotent and omniscient; that is, his duration reaches from eternity to eternity; his presence from infinity to infinity.

—Sir Isaac Newton, *Principia*, translation by Andrew Motte

Inhabitants of time that we are, we stand with one foot in eternity. God, as Isaiah says (57:15) "inhabiteth eternity" but stands with one foot in time. The part of time where he stands most particularly is Christ, and thus in Christ we catch a glimpse of what eternity is all about, what God is all about, and what we ourselves are all about too.

—Frederick Buechner, *Wishful Thinking*

Every bit of love and beauty and truth that anyone ever experiences on earth is made in heaven and is a participation in heaven. For heaven is God's presence; and God is present in all goodness, all truth, and all beauty. God is not a truth, a good, a beauty, but Goodness Itself and Truth Itself and Beauty Itself.

—Peter J. Kreeft, *Heaven*

The privilege of being with Christ in heaven, where he sits on the throne, as the King of angels, and the God of the universe; shining forth as the Sun of that world of Glory;—there to dwell in the full, constant, and everlasting view of his beauty and brightness;—there most freely and intimately to converse with him, and fully to enjoy his love, as his friends and brethren; there to share with him in the infinite pleasure and joy which he has in the enjoyment of his Father;—there to sit with him on his throne, to reign with him in the possession of all things, to partake with him in the glory of his victory over his enemies, and the advancement of his kingdom in the world, and to join with him in joyful songs of praise to his Father and our Father, to his God and our God, for ever and ever? Is not this a privilege worth the seeking after?

—Jonathan Edwards, "Funeral Sermon for David Brainerd"

Heaven is the place where God is specially present, in that he works there more richly and revealingly, bestowing his presence by a more obvious and visible providence than on earth, by a more abundant grace, causing those present to be transparent to his glory and love.

—Peter Toon, *Heaven and Hell*

There to dwell in the full, constant, and everlasting view of his beauty and brightness.

I SAW THE HOLY CITY

Godfrey Thring

I saw the holy city,
  The New Jerusalem,
Come down from heaven, a bride adorned
  With jeweled diadem;
The flood of crystal waters
  Flowed down the golden street;
And nations brought their honours there,
  And laid them at her feet.

And there no sun was needed,
  Nor moon to shine by night,
God's glory did enlighten all,
  The Lamb himself the light;
And there his servants serve him,
  And, life's long battle o'er,
Enthroned with him, their Saviour, King,
  They reign for evermore.

O great and glorious vision!
  The Lamb upon his throne;
O wondrous sight for man to see!
  The Saviour with his own:
To drink the living waters
  And stand upon the shore,
Where neither sorrow, sin, nor death
  Shall ever enter more.

RESOUNDING PRAISE

I looked and saw a Lamb standing there before the twenty-four Elders, in front of the throne and the Living Beings, and on the Lamb were wounds that once had caused his death. . . .

Then in my vision I heard the singing of millions of angels surrounding the throne and the Living Beings and the Elders: "The Lamb is worthy" (loudly they sang it!) "—the Lamb who was slain. He is worthy to receive the power, and the riches, and the wisdom, and the strength, and the honor, and the glory, and the blessing."

And then I heard everyone in heaven and earth, and from the dead beneath the earth and in the sea, exclaiming, "The blessing and the honor and the glory and the power belong to the one sitting on the throne, and to the Lamb forever and ever."

—Revelation 5:6, 11-13 (TLB)

But O, the strains, how full and clear,
  Of that eternal choir!

—John Ellerton

"The blessing and the honor and the glory and the power belong to the one sitting on the throne, and to the Lamb forever and ever."

and that will be heaven

and that will be heaven
at last   the first unclouded
seeing
          to stand like the sunflower
turned full face to the sun   drenched
with light   in the still centre
held   while the circling planets
hum with an utter joy

          seeing and knowing
at last   in every particle
seen and known
               and not turning
away
          never turning away
again

—Evangeline Paterson

The development of spirituality, the growth of our life in God, flows naturally into a life with God after death, the kind of life in which we will see God and know Him in the same way He knows and loves us, a life in which we share with Jesus the eternal ecstasy of God's presence and the joyful and endless companionship of God's family and our own loved ones whom God has called home.

—Joseph F. Girzone, *Never Alone*

The life of heaven is the inexhaustible fountain of God's thought and God's love.

—Peter J. Kreeft, *Heaven*

When we've been there ten thousand years,
Bright shining as the sun,
We've no less days to sing God's praise
Than when we first begun.

—from "Amazing Grace," John Newton

Thy praise shall never, never fail Throughout eternity.

Crown Him with Many Crowns

Crown him the Lord of years,
  The Potentate of time,
Creator of the rolling spheres,
  Ineffably sublime!

Glassed in a sea of light
  Whose everlasting waves
Reflect his form—the Infinite!
  Who lives, and loves, and saves.

Crown him the Lord of Heaven!
  One with the Father known,—
And blest Spirit, through him given
  From yonder Triune throne!

His glories now we sing,
  Who died and rose on high,
Who died eternal life to bring,
  And lives that death may die.

All hail! Redeemer, hail!
  For thou hast died for me:
Thy praise shall never, never fail
  Throughout eternity.

—Matthew Bridges and Godfrey Thring

Where light, and life, and joy, and peace
  In undivided empire reign,
And thronging angels never cease
  Their deathless strain;

Where saints are clothed in spotless white
  And evening shadows never fall,
Where thou, eternal Light of Light,
  Art Lord of all.

—Godfrey Thring

Praise, my soul, the King of heaven;
  To his feet thy tribute bring;
Ransomed, healed, restored, forgiven,
  Evermore his praises sing:
    Alleluia! Alleluia!
  Praise the everlasting King.

Angels in the height, adore him!
  Ye behold him face to face;
Saints triumphant bow before him!
  Gathered in from every race.
    Alleluia! Alleluia!
  Praise with us the God of grace.

—Henry F. Lyte

ARRIVAL

Angels gather.
The rush of mad air
cyclones through.
Wing tips brush the
hair, a million
strands
stand; waving black anemones.
Hosannahs crush the
shell's ear tender, and
tremble
down clattering
to the floor.
Harps sound,
undulate their
sensuous meanings.
Hallelujah! Hallelujah!
You
beyond the door.

—Maya Angelou, *Shaker, Why Don't You Sing?*

THIS GRAND CRESCENDO
Rebecca Ruter Springer
from "My Dream of Heaven"

I walked slowly down into the water, and soon found myself floating in mid-current. The wonderful prismatic rays that in early morning were such a marvel, now blended into a golden glory, with different shades of rose and purple flashing athwart their splendor. To me it seemed even more beautiful than the rainbow tints; just as the maturer joys of our earthly life cast into shadow, somewhat, the more evanescent pleasures of youth. I could but wonder what its evening glories would be, and resolved to come at some glowing twilight, and see if they would not remind me of the calm hours of life's closing day. I heard the chimes from the silver bell of the great city ringing an anthem, and its notes seemed to chant clearly;

> "Holy! Holy! Holy! Lord God Almighty!" The waters took up the song and a thousand waves about me responded, "Holy! Holy! Holy!"

The notes seemed to "vibrate" upon the waves, producing a wondrously harmonious effect. The front row in the battalion of advancing waves softly chanted "Holy" as they passed onward; immediately the second roll of waves took up the word that the first seemed to have dropped as it echoed the second "Holy" in the divine chorus, then it, too, passed onward to take up the second note as the third advancing column caught the first; and so it passed and echoed from wave to wave, until it seemed millions of tiny waves about me had taken up and were bearing their part in this grand crescendo—this wonderful anthem.

In heaven's eternal bliss
The loveliest strain is this,
*   May Jesus Christ be praised;*
Let earth, and sea, and sky
From depth to height reply,
*   May Jesus Christ be praised.*

—Anonymous, translation by Edward Caswell

TAMBOURINES!
Langston Hughes

Tambourines!
Tambourines!
Tambourines!
To the glory of God!
Tambourines
To glory!

A gospel shout
And a gospel song:
Life is short
But God is long!

Tambourines!
Tambourines!
Tambourines!
To glory!

PRAYERS

O God, who on the mount didst reveal to chosen witnesses thine only-begotten Son wonderfully transfigured, in raiment white and glistering: Mercifully grant that we, being delivered from the disquietude of this world, may be permitted to behold the King in his beauty; who with thee O Father, and thee O Holy Ghost, liveth and reigneth one God, world without end.

—William Reed Huntington

O Father, gracious was that word which clos'd
Thy sovereign sentence that Man should find grace;
For which both Heav'n and Earth shall high extoll
Thy praises, with th' innumerable sound
Of Hymns and sacred Songs, wherewith thy Throne
Encompass'd shall resound thee ever blest.

—John Milton, *Paradise Lost*, adapted

O Father, gracious was that word which clos'd Thy sovereign sentence that Man should find grace.

In heaven I shall live without wearying;
  there rejoice without grief;
  there delight without being sated;
  and there, loving you, seeing you, glorying in you,
  shall be satisfied for ever.
For truly my treasure is you, yourself.

—Richard Rolle, *The Fire of Love*, translation by Clifton Wolters, adapted